$11.95

# 75 YEARS WITH THE SHOTGUN

*A right and left on quail with a double retrieve by Sport and Tex made the day complete for the author.*

# 75 YEARS WITH THE SHOTGUN

by C. T. "BUCK" BUCKMAN

An expert hunter and trapshooter shares experiences of a lifetime.

1974 • VALLEY PUBLISHERS • FRESNO, CALIFORNIA

COPYRIGHT 1974

by

Valley Publishers

Library of Congress Card Number 74-75804

ISBN 0-913548-18-9

Printed in the United States of America

Dedicated to my wife Edna and my daughter Lois who spent many lonesome days and nights while I was at the duck club or otherwise following my hobby.

# Acknowledgements

I would like to express my thanks to all the fine men and women, ranch owners, cattlemen, property owners, orchardists, vineyardists and others, who have so kindly given me permission to hunt on their property.

It has been very gratifying because otherwise I would have been unable to enjoy all the fine days in the field over the past 75 years. Thanks so much.

I want to thank Joseph E. Doctor for all his help and advice during my writings and for his prodding to keep me at it! To Charley Dickey, recent head of the National Shooting Sports Foundation, Inc., for permitting me to use his writings. To William E. Rae, Editor-in-Chief of *Outdoor Life*, for the use of the article regarding Sport and the quail shoot at Shandon, California. To Ian "Ike" McMillan and Mrs. McMillan for all their kindness and courtesies during my various visits to their ranch and for the guest chapter "Quail Hunting, for Sportsmen Only." To Glen E. Robertson, Instructor at the College of Sequoias, for his counsel and advice. To Anna Savage, owner of the Superior Secretarial Service, for her patience during the preparation of the various transcripts. To Annie Mitchell for her proof-reading of the final manuscript and her constructive criticism thereof. All of these people I thank from the bottom of my heart. There may be others I have forgotten, but to them I must apologize. It is an error of the head and not of the heart. Sincerely,

C. T. Buckman

# Introduction

For many years I have had the desire to put into writing my various experiences with upland game hunting. Recently my desires have become almost an obsession. So I have made myself try my hand. Perhaps I may leave an idea for the boy of tomorrow.

Permit me to quote a piece of poetry that has always been close to my heart and has a deft meaning from which others may get some satisfaction. It was written by Gelett Burgess, a fine California poet who passed away in San Francisco some years ago. It is entitled:

### BALLADE OF CONCEIT

To all ye critics who come to chill
  And to smirch the work of the blessed few
Who feed on the fancy they try to kill,
  I snap my fingers -- the sapless crew!

What do I care if they bark and mew?
  This is the teeth of the mouths that whine;
What have ye wrought ye can say this to:
  "By Jove, I made it, and it is mine."

Never a book that was writ so ill,
  Never a picture so false of hue
Never a song with so little thrill
  That it had not something I'm glad was true!

What if I fail? I can still pursue
  Joy of Creation, the gift divine!
And he who creates has at least this view:
  "By Jove, I made it, and it is mine!"

Thank God, who gave me the wits and will,
   And the raging passion to put it through,
I never saw task that took so much skill
   I dared not try, and I cared not to!

My work is crude, and a bit askew,
   You're free to condemn it, line by line,
But, bred of my brain, in my heart it grew;
   "By Jove, I made it, and it is mine!"

### ENVOY

Critics, your parasite life renew;
   Drink my conceit, for it flows like wine;
Here is my poem and here is your cue!
   "By Jove, I made it, and it is mine!"

With the above in mind, I am going to do what I have wanted to do for these many years. Remember, young men, it will not be done unless you attempt to do it. Then, "It can be done."

# Foreword

The shotgun is -- and has been since the invention of gunpowder -- an instrument of amazing versatility. According, of course, to the nature and intent of the individual who presses it to his shoulder.

It is so fearsomely lethal that it has been outlawed as a weapon of war; chief persuader in the arsenal of the lawman and the outlaw in the American West, it killed more men than the sixgun and the repeating rifle combined. It has quelled riots and set the hearts of fierce desperadoes to quaking. Its gaping black tunnel of death has been the last earthly object of view to many a victim.

In the forests and on the plains of Europe, Asia and the Americas it has often been a prime provider of succulent game for the tables of rich and poor; it came west in the wagons of the American pioneers and the old double-barrelled hammer guns of yesterday are treasures of antiquarians. The shotgun killed large or small game, according to the load, buckshot or birdshot, with equal facility, and it did not take expert marksmanship to register a kill.

To the elite of Europe, it was a sporting weapon in the field. No doubt many a diplomatic coup or decision of state was scored by men who established manly convivial rapport shooting game birds on an upland moor behind good dogs and finely crafted shotguns. Even in days when conservationists have scored heavily, there is little disagreement that many game species sufficiently propagate, and are sufficiently protected, to provide wholesome sport for the shooter for a long time to come.

It is with the shotgun as a sporting implement that this book is concerned. Its author is an ideal person to prepare such a book. He has had more than 75 years of shotgunning, both as a hunter and a tournament competitor, and he is still at it at the age of 84. Let's meet this man.

Clement T. Buckman is the founder and Chairman of the Board of a successful 57-year-old insurance agency in Visalia, a prosperous community located in California's fertile San Joaquin Valley and in close proximity to some of the most diverse and excellent upland game and waterfowl shooting in the world.

Buck, as his friends know him, is the third Clement T. His grandfather, who bore the name, was a Kentuckian who came west as the captain of a wagon train in the early 1850's. He attempted to settle in Arizona, but the Indians drove him out. He ended up with a small farm east of Visalia. His son, the second Clement T., left the farm as a young man, moved to Visalia where he married Irene Combs, member of a pioneer family, and entered politics. After serving as justice of the peace and county auditor, he moved to nearby Exeter and established himself, despite the loss of an arm in a hunting accident, as a skilled teamster on precipitous mountain roads, including the hair-raising one leading to Mineral King.

His son, the present Clement T., was born in Visalia and grew to manhood with a rugged physique. In high school Buck played halfback on the football team and catcher on the baseball team. He has maintained a lifelong interest in nearly all sports.

Buck wanted to go to college, but there were no family resources and athletic scholarships were practically unknown. Instead, he learned surveying, then the equivalent of civil engineering, by taking a correspondence course and receiving tutoring from friends. He made a surveying field trip to Oregon and later qualified for a California surveying license. He hung out his shingle in the newly incorporated little city of Exeter, whose first city "engineer" he became.

One day Buck bought an insurance policy and shortly thereafter began moonlighting as a salesman for the company from whom he bought the policy. One rainy day when he could not practice surveying, he sold five policies, revealing that he not only had sales talent, but also that it could make him more money than his transit. He gave up surveying, moved to Visalia, and built the thriving insurance business he still heads.

In 1912, Buck married a young lady from a pioneer family, Edna Tschumy. Today he has a grandson, Stanley Simpson, associated with him in business, and three great-granddaughters.

Buck cannot remember when he fired his first charge of shot. Like most rural western boys, he grew up with guns. He had plenty of opportunity on the plains and in the foothills and high country of the Sierra Nevada to shoot game of all kinds, and he loved it.

"It isn't how many birds you get," he said. "It is being out there with a smart dog and good companions. If you get 10 birds, that is incidental."

One day in the 1930's some friends invited Buck to a trapshooting range they had built. He broke only nine birds out of his first 50. He soon acquired the knack and henceforth took a delight in competitive shooting, and the tougher the competition, the better he enjoys it.

"I like it best when I am tied with another shooter. Then I really get going."

He won the San Joaquin Valley doubles championship in 1932 and the California State championship in 1946. He has competed all over America, even in the Grand American.

Buck modestly believes that other shooters will enjoy vicariously some of his experiences, and that young shooters especially may benefit from the knowledge he has acquired. Shooters or not, readers will enjoy the spirited way he says his say.

Joseph E. Doctor

## Table of Contents

| | | |
|---|---|---|
| 1 | A Good Teacher | 1 |
| 2 | Shotguns | 3 |
| 3 | Ethics of Hunting | 9 |
| 4 | A Southern Gentleman | 15 |
| 5 | The Quail Call | 19 |
| 6 | Quail Hunting, For Sportsmen Only | 22 |
| 7 | On the San Miguel | 27 |
| 8 | Mountain Quail | 30 |
| 9 | Bobwhite Quail | 33 |
| 10 | I Learn About Quail | 39 |
| 11 | Trapshooting | |
| 12 | Setters | 62 |
| 13 | Dove Shooting | 67 |
| 14 | Whitewings | 76 |
| 15 | Bandtail Pigeons | 81 |
| 16 | An Oregon Shoot | 88 |
| 17 | Grouse and Hungarian Partridge | 92 |
| 18 | Wild Turkey | 104 |
| 19 | Sage Hen or the Sage Grouse | 108 |
| 20 | Wilson Snipe | 112 |
| 21 | Upland Plover | 115 |
| 22 | Sandhill Cranes | 118 |
| 23 | Rambling Memories | 121 |
| 24 | Clubs and Shooting Preserves | 129 |
| Appendix   A Few Recipes | | 133 |

# 1 | A Good Teacher

I cannot remember my earliest day in the field. I do remember helping my father load the brass shells before I was old enough to carry a gun. It was one of the greatest thrills of my life to watch him shoot because at the early age of 16 he had the misfortune to lose his right arm between the elbow and the shoulder. Yes, he lost it while training a bird dog and on a quail shoot. He had leaned the gun against the fence and then helped the young setter through the wire. The dog knocked the gun over and, as those were the days before the safety lock, it exploded. His arm went with it.

Some months later, while sitting on the front porch of the ranch house with my grandfather, a covey of quail flew into the field immediately adjoining the yard. Grandfather said, "Son, get your gun and get me a few quail." Without hesitation, Dad did just that. He switched to his left shoulder, held the gun up with the stub of his right arm and got some quail for not only my grandfather but for the whole family. Years later, when I helped him load the old brass shells and afterwards, his teachings were on two main subjects pertaining to hunting: safety and sportsmanship.

You can well imagine that Father was more than ordinarily careful with a shotgun and that he used every known method to impart the knowledge that he had learned the hard way to one of his young sons. Incidentally, Dad could do anything with his one arm except perhaps wheel a wheelbarrow. I will tell you later of how I found out he could use his left arm.

The nearest I can remember of a serious accident was with J. Thomas Crowe, one of Visalia's prominent attorneys. We were hunting quail in a vineyard, near Sultana. It was early in the fall and the vines had not been pruned, so the canes were sticking up hither and thither. The quail flushed. I knew where my partner was located and, it being my shot, I fired. One number eight shot hit a vine cane, glanced off at an angle of some 40 degrees and hit Crowe on the forehead. He let out a yell. I ran over and apologized with the additional statement that one does not get the opportunity to shoot a white Crowe but once in his lifetime.

A few of the things Dad taught me regarding safety will not be amiss, at least to the young men who may read these lines and who will be the sportsmen of tomorrow. Remember this, never point a gun at anything you do not want to kill. I have found that if you will use a light gun and carry it pointing upward you will never harm anything should it explode accidentally. I have also found out that you can lower the gun for shooting position as fast as raising the gun for a shot. Speed is all important in quail shooting because our California quail can surely put a rock, a tree or a bush between you and itself in seconds.

Always remove shells from the gun when crossing a fence. It is well to break the gun, lay it on the ground and then crawl through the fence yourself. You do not want the experience that Dad had or it may be much more serious.

Another must while hunting is to always know the exact position of your hunting partner regardless of the cover in which you are hunting. One would never get over knowing that one was the cause of an injury to a friend. Many safety rules have been given to the shooting fraternity by ammunition and gun companies. It will not be necessary to repeat them. The above rules, drilled into me by my father, may save a life or, at least, a serious injury.

# 2 | Shotguns

My earliest memories of shotguns concern the three double barrels owned by my father -- one, a D. H. E. Parker Brothers, another an L. C. Smith and the third, a Lefever. All were 12 gauges and comparatively light guns, because Dad had but one arm, and a heavy gun was hard for him to handle. Smaller gauge guns were probably made, but they were not used or owned in this area. As I grew older, he gave me the Parker and was I a proud young man! I liked the Lefever, probably due to its balance which means so much in a shotgun.

I will never forget our last shoot together, in what was known as the Blain field on the north side of the Yokohl Valley, some 15 miles east of Exeter, California. We had a fine covey of quail in cover in the ravine, with Dad on one side and me on the other. It was beautiful shooting, with my dog Sport pointing and steady as a rock. I watched Father just smother about 20 birds, with the air full of feathers, but not a bird hit the ground. My heart went out to him. I suggested that we had enough birds and that we go home. He agreed, so we put our guns in their cases and returned home. He passed away soon thereafter.

His gift made a Parker Brothers fan out of me. I have shot them for 60 years in the field and believe it to be America's finest shotgun. To me, it balances and it never shoots loose. At least one has never shot loose for me.

There were, and are, other good American-built shotguns; namely, the L. C. Smith, the Ithaca, the Remington and the Lefever, as well as the Baker; but for my money I'll take the

Parker Brothers! All these mentioned are double barrel shotguns. I will discuss the repeating shotguns later in this chapter.

While I tried other makes of guns than the Parker, I have always returned to my first love. After I once loaned my beloved 12 gauge that Dad had given me, and the borrower got some leaves in the barrel and blew the gun up, I tried a 16 gauge. Incidentally, let me admonish any sportsman that there are two things not to loan, provided you love them: your shotgun and your wife. I tried the 16 for a year or two, but for some reason it did not fill the bill. So, I had a little idea of my own. I would get a 20 gauge and perhaps I could get Mrs. Buckman to go hunting with me, figuring she could handle smaller and lighter guns.

I saved my money and made the purchase, a beautiful little D. H. E. Parker Brothers' 20 gauge. It weighed about 5½ pounds. The season came around and Mrs. Buckman promised to go. One day we loaded up and went down to the Rice Ranch, south of Farmersville. We drove into the yard, so help me, there was a covey of some 200 birds waiting for us. I put the two guns together and looked for the 20 gauge shells; again, so help me, I had forgotten them. I have never lived that down and Mrs. Buckman has never gone hunting with me or learned to shoot.

I later sold the 16 and used the 20 gauge. I shot the 20 for several years, until I learned of the 28 Parker, which I purchased and have used ever since.

Some years ago I learned of an A-1 Special 28 gauge Parker with two sets of barrels, owned by a Mr. W. O. Rowley in Dallas, Texas. I called him by phone and it was for sale, but he wanted $3,000 for it, and that amount does not grow on trees. However, the more time passed, the more I wanted that gun. I spent over $80 telephoning Rowley and finally, with a healthy deposit, he sent it to me on approval. When it came I knew it was a sale and that I was going to be the owner of an A-1 Special 28 gauge Parker with two sets of barrels. It was in perfect condition, just like it had never been shot, and was I happy! Here was the ultimate in a Parker shotgun.

My friends and shooting partners thought I had gone nuts and told me so. I frankly told them that it was my money I was spending, that it would not break me and that it would not cause Mrs. Buckman to go without dinner or any other meal. It was a beautiful gun and I had a great deal of pleasure from it over a period of several years.

One day Steve Billeci walked into my office and said, "Buck, I want that 28 gauge Parker of yours." I answered, after a moment's thought, "Steve, just how damn bad do you want that gun?" He knew what I had paid for it, so looked me right in the eye and said, "Buck, I'll give you $4,500 for it."

I hesitated a moment and came right back with, "Steve, you just bought a shotgun." With that he peeled off 15 one-hundred-dollar bills, sat down and wrote me a check for $3,000 and handed me the sum total. I reported and paid my capital gains tax. The sad part of the deal was that he had but a short time to enjoy his purchase. He passed to the great beyond some few months later. I later sold it for Mrs. Billeci to the president of the Keiser Electronics Corporation for exactly what Mr. Billeci had paid for the gun, so neither Steve Billeci nor Buckman had been altogether crazy. It was a beautiful showpiece and I doubt if there were, or ever had been, ten in existence.

While on the subject of 28 gauge shotguns, let me say something about this size gun and give you my reasons for using it in the field. By all odds, the 28 gauge should be as extinct as the passenger pigeon, but it is making something of a comeback. In addition, it is continuing as a class in skeet shooting.

At one time almost every American gun company manufactured a shotgun of this gauge, but they soon faded out for some unknown reason when the European gunmakers from Spain, France, Belgium, England and Italy took over and furnished some better than fair guns. Not a Parker like I had become used to using, but of course these were now getting almost impossible to come by and their prices were getting unreasonable.

Two of the most interesting models from Europe and available here in the United States were the French Darne double, sold by Stoeger Arms Corporation and an Italian over-and-under made especially for Abercrombie and Fitch, as well as a light over-and-under made in Japan for the Daley people. I am presently shooting one of these guns, and it is giving satisfactory service.

Now they are not being turned out on a light frame. The new heavy frame Daley does not have the balance that the lighter gun possesses.

These guns weigh anywhere from 4½ pounds to just under six pounds in the Parker, but the Parker is so well balanced that it feels much lighter.

This brings us to the real reason for the continued existence of 28 gauge guns that are light to carry all day long, that point like a flash at quick-flushing birds like quail, or fast-flying birds like doves, and are still comfortable to shoot. Far better quail hunters than I have been convinced that light guns and light loads make for far greater pleasure and more game in the bag when hunting these magnificent little birds.

Too many of us go quail or dove shooting with big seven- to eight-pound 12 gauge guns, fill them with high brass shells, shooting 1¼ to 1⅜ ounce loads. These are guns and shells for duck and goose hunters, trying, usually in vain, to make a 50- to 70-yard kill.

Most quail and doves are killed from a distance of between 20 and 25 yards. Some in heavy cover must be grassed even closer before they get out of sight. We must shoot fast if we expect to have a few for dinner. With that in mind, why do we go after them with guns that weigh half again as much as they should and why do we use shells which are most likely to blow the birds to bits? I suppose we continue to do so because 12 gauge must be better because it is bigger, and magnum shells must be more deadly because they also have more everything, including powder, shot, recoil and price. This, my friends, is the reason why the 28 gauge guns of good quality bring premium prices today. One can carry one all day without becoming arm-weary, and even when the last covey flushes, just before sunset, we can still get on them like a flash.

I don't say that the 28 gauge gun is the only all-purpose gun or shell. If there is such a thing, it is probably the 20 gauge, but with the standard ¾-ounce load, the 28 gauge is a first-class quail and dove gun. Possibly the best. With either the ⅞-ounce or one-ounce of shot, it will serve to perfection the man who is a reasonably good shot and does a lot of walking hunting pheasants; therefore, glad to have a light and fast gun.

If you have always thought of the 28 gauge as either too small or as an orphan, try one sometime on fast-flushing game birds, either quail, dove or pheasants, and see if it doesn't lighten your step while making your game bag heavier. If enough of us adopt this effective gauge, it will never become extinct.

When one is thinking of shotguns, one must consider the very fine double guns manufactured in England by Wesley Richards, Purdy, Holland and Holland, WW Greener and the Fracotte from Belgium, and the Beretta from Italy, as well as the Sauer from Germany, and the less expensive doubles from Spain.

Remember, all good double guns are hand made. Labor is the reason we in the United States had to quit building fine guns like Parker, Smith, Ithaca, Remington and others over the last 30 years, and it is also the reason that the fine guns of England have gone up in price to where so many sportsmen have gone to pumps and automatics, which are run through a machine and produced in quantity, something that cannot be done with a good double.

The repeating shotgun is an American invention. The old Spencer is credited with being the first pump gun. The Model Ninety-Three Winchester was one of the first that I remember, followed by the Winchester Model Ninety-Seven, which was a fine duck gun and, incidentally, was used by Frank Troeh, of Portland, Oregon, for years for his trapshooting. He won championship after championship, nationwide, with his old Winchester Ninety-Seven.

Many hunters prefer the single barrel pump or automatic, but I was raised on a double. They are just a finer built piece of equipment. One must plug a pump or automatic now, so they do not have the advantage of additional shots. Dad used to say to me, "If you can't get them with two shots, let them go."

I must tell you about a visit I made to London. When the party was going to the Shakespeare country, I reneged and would not go. I stayed in London and visited the big gun factories. It was a revelation to see those Englishmen polish that steel to make it fit and see them do the beautiful checkering. No wonder a good English gun costs what it does, and that is probably why I bought and still shoot a Webly and Scott 28 gauge double.

# 3 | Ethics of Hunting

Author -- Anonymous

Probably the most important item in a day afield is your shooting partner. Hunting is for fun and that is impossible with a selfish, boorish, or dangerous shooting companion.

Choose your shooting companion with the greatest of care, and measure yourself by the same standards.

If he is a casual acquaintance who sometimes irks you in the usual haunts of business or society, you can bet that his true spirit will blossom in the field when the going gets rough. A shooting companion should be a good friend, whose true virtues are known to you and whom you know can take it under stress.

Choose a hunting partner according to the intensity of his interest. Some men do most of their hunting over a cup of coffee; others are intense with their whole heart and soul, who will hang tough until the sun goes down. Determine the degree of your own interest and then get with your partners.

Gun sense is important in a hunting companion. You can hand a gun to a man and find out in no uncertain terms what his total experience is in a very few minutes. The real hunter handles a gun with reverence, assurance, ease and respect. He knows the gun. You owe it to yourself and your family to side with such a man and you owe it to him to return in kind.

A shoot may be a grim trial to be endured or a dream to remember. In either case, it is a mutual understanding and undertaking to be shared without selfishness -- sharing shooting opportunities, hunting techniques, food, equipment, water and something of each other. It must never be seriously competitive. No good thing should be hogged by one man. The only place for selfishness on a hunt is hogging more than your share of the work, discomfort and disappointment.

There may be times when Lady Luck and Mother Nature, a pair of fickle old jades at best, team up against you. A predicted sprinkle becomes an all-day rain. You hunt every cover but the right one, or your dog does everything but what he should do. A good partner expects such things and accepts the unchangeable with grace. He can endure adversity and can grin off a case of creeping irritation.

And in his eyes how do you stack up?

Maybe you're cold, hungry or tired. You do not have to dwell on it; your partner probably feels the same way. If you honestly feel that you shouldn't or can't go on, face it frankly and cheerfully, but don't whine. Whining will ruin everyone's day and stamp you as a gutless wonder who has no business afield.

One of the gravest offenses against a companion is to betray his confidence and spread the word about his personal covers and hunting grounds. He has spent too much effort and time finding a place to shoot to have you take your friends out to shoot it out. If a man thinks enough of you to share his prized secrets, respect that confidence. Such places are meant to be shared between you and him and not be usurped by others.

Nearly as bad is the claimer who shoots and grabs and hotly denies ever missing a shot. There may be times when the issue of who killed a bird may honestly be in doubt. If so, waive your claim. No game, not even a trophy, is worth risking a friendship.

A real hunting partner is one who shares without asking a share in return, who gives without thinking, who places your well being and pleasure above his own.

Such a man may be rich and well born, or a smelly old duffer in overalls, but mark him well wherever you find him. He is a gentleman and a proper man to share your hunting.

## What Is a Quail Hunter?*

By Charley Dickey
Manager
National Shooting Sports Foundation

Between a boy's first shotgun and a tottering old man we find a delightfully unpredictable creature called a quail hunter. Quail hunters come in assorted sizes, but all of them have the same creed: To enjoy every second of every minute of every hour of every hunting trip -- and to violently protest when the sun sinks beneath the horizon and it gets too dark to hunt.

Quail hunters are found nearly everywhere -- on steep ridges, bragging in offices, field trials, swamps, sporting goods stores, conservation meetings, Sunday Schools, back rooms and at board meetings. Mothers love them, young girls hate them, older brothers and sisters tolerate them, the boss envies them, and Heaven protects them. A quail hunter is Truth with dirt on its face, Beauty with a briar scratch on its finger, Wisdom with Nature as its God, and the Hope of the future with good will toward man.

When you are busy, a quail hunter is thinking of pointers, setters and country roads. When you want him to make a good impression on a client, he may talk only of the triple he once bagged, the way Ole Spot honors a point, the spring bird hatch or the prospects of his newest pup.

A quail hunter is a composite -- he is content with "rat" cheese and crackers for lunch at a country store but his ulcer has to be pampered with a special lunch when he's home; he

*Based on Alan Beck's "What is a Boy?"

will drink from any old well without question; he has the energy of a hurricane when he starts hunting although in the office it tires him to walk to the pay window; he has the lungs of a dictator when he yells at the dogs, although his secretary complains that he whispers all the time; he has the imagination of a scientist as he looks for coveys along each likely hedge; he shows the audacity of a steel trap as he tramps through green briars oblivious of the pain in his thighs; he has the enthusiasm of a firecracker as he beats every brush pile, and when the dogs go on point, he has forgotten to load his gun.

He likes dirty hunting pants, old guns, hunting knives, leaky boots, long weekends, all kinds of field dogs, back roads, wool shirts, abandoned farms and questionable companions who also are quail hunters. He is not much for social gatherings between Thanksgiving and March, stray cats, neckties, educational books, weekend company, barbers, people who post land, and clients who don't hunt. Without thought of race, creed or color, he likes people who hunt bobwhite quail three months a year and talk about it twelve.

Nobody else is so early to rise, or so late to supper -- during the bird season. Nobody else gets so much fun out of chasing dogs, trampling honeysuckle, and getting mud on his feet. Nobody else suffers so silently with aching feet, twisted ankles and strained muscles. Nobody else can cram into one pocket a rusty knife, 17 No. 8 shells, an extra pack of smokes, a compass that doesn't work, six dog biscuits, change for lunch, a hunting license, waterproof matches, extra boot laces, a broken dog whistle, a snake-bite kit, and a bottle opener.

A quail hunter is a magical creature -- you might get sore at his constant chatter about birds but you can't lock him out of your heart. You can assign him itineraries in the spring, but you know where he'll be in the fall. His sales chart will be as good as the next, but he'll get it there in his own sweet time.

## What Is a Quail Hunter?

He may be the very one who sells the "rich old buzzard" who spends his winters quail hunting in Georgia.

You might as well give up -- the quail hunter is a child of Nature with a hopeless one-track mind. He'll do his work with the best of them, but when December rolls around he's out in the field behind a young pup and an old veteran on the prowl for Mr. Bobwhite. He's earnest in his work but he's just a little more sincere when he's slow-trailing a jumpy covey.

And though you get sore at him in the winter, you know you'll always like him. There's something about him that rings true -- he's almost too honest. He's a simple and kindly man who asks no more of life than that the birds fly fast, the dogs hold tight, and everything has a sporting chance to live or die.

*Peggy was a quail dog but she brought the grouse to me by dragging it up the hill. It was new to her. (See chapter on grouse.)*

# 4 | A Southern Gentleman

In the early Thirties, it was my privilege to make the acquaintance of Joe Terry, a representative of the Winchester Arms Company in the San Joaquin Valley. Terry was a southern gentleman from Alabama and, of course, an ardent bird shooter. He shot targets and made most of the registered shoots in his territory. It was during a conversation at one of these shoots that we got on the subject of quail hunting, as we call it. In the South they say bird shooting. He expressed a desire to shoot in our area, and I extended an invitation. I was pretty smug about what I knew about quail and about quail hunting, but you may remember the expression "I learned about women from her." To paraphrase that saying, I got some very valuable pointers from Terry.

Some months later, on a Saturday morning, the telephone rang and it was Terry's southern voice saying, "Hello Buck, let's go bird shooting." Never needing an excuse to go hunting, I said, "Okay, boy, where are you? I'll pick you up in 45 minutes."

All the arrangements made, I changed my clothes and met Joe at his friend's home at the appointed time. In those days we could find a covey of birds near town in almost any direction. Out near where the trap grounds are located we found the birds along the old slough running through the Smith property. We got permission from Clinton and Leslie Smith, as I knew we would because of a long-standing friendship from high school days.

It was not easy shooting. The birds were in fairly heavy cover along the bank. I was in the dry bottom working the dog. Terry did not have one and I had one of my three outstanding setters. This was my first. It was a spayed bitch called Peggy. I was beating the brush with a long stick. Terry was on the bank. We were getting quite a little shooting, but Terry was having his troubles. I was not doing much better, with a stick in one hand and a gun in the other.

He, I knew, was a pretty fair shot, and only shooting about 20 percent. It was very close shooting with willows on each bank. Finally after another miss, Terry said, "Buck, let's go to town. I want to change guns." We did just that. He did not change guns, but we did change the barrel. He had been shooting a full choke barrel in this close shooting, and it was just not his day.

We had lunch and drove down to the Combs Ranch southeast of town, now called the Linda Loma Ranch and owned by the Jenan Brothers. After getting the information, we headed north to the slough, hoping to find the birds there in the weeds on the south side, but without my usual luck. They were on the north side in a peach orchard and quite a covey, perhaps 100 to 150 birds. When they flushed, I shot into the air to scare them, to make them go to cover, which was unnecessary here because they flew to the fence line covered with blackberry briers and I remarked that the jig was up, that we may as well go find another covey.

Terry said, "No, we may be able to get out some," and it was there that the saying "I learned about women from her" came in very appropriately. I learned something about quail hunting from Terry.

He said "Over thar, Buck." I got over to the fence and he started to slowly whistle like a crippled quail and those birds started coming out one or two at a time, first on my side and then on his side. We had perhaps a half a dozen when he stopped and said, "This old improved cylinder is the barrel for this game," and it surely was. He was now shooting nearly 80 or 90 percent, and I was right with him.

The birds that we did not shoot at flew east along the fence line into another berry patch, and I knew they would be harder to get out this time, but we went after them. He again said, "Over thar, Buck." I was ready this time, and we got in position. He stood out some 15 or 20 feet, reaching into his hunting coat pocket and pulled out, of all things, a package of firecrackers, touched them to a cigarette he was smoking and tossed them into the patch of blackberries.

Boy, the birds started out and we finished our day's shoot with limits right there! I had learned something about quail from Terry, and it has come in mighty handy on many occasions in the hills where the birds go to cover in the rock piles. One must be careful, however, not to use the fireworks when the grass is dry, but the whistle will almost always work and can be learned with a little observation.

It was a year or two later that I was invited to shoot ducks with a friend at his Los Banos club. He got me to my blind and soon thereafter a messenger came out for him to go to town. He left me and promised to come after me about 10:30. I was on my own, and I was not having too much luck. I had a very few of various kinds, but I witnessed the sprig going into a blind north of me. After an hour or two, the shooting stopped and the shooter picked up his birds, put them on his strap and started down the levee toward me. I waited, and who would it be? Joe Terry.

I said, "Hello, Joe," and he came back with "Of all things, Buck." We chatted for a few minutes. He found out that I had not had too much luck, so he invited me to go back to his blind and he would try his calling whistle. He surely worked that sprig whistle. He brought the sprig in singles and pairs, and I had the shoot of my life. It was a revelation to see him call sprigs, which to me is one of the finest wildfowl. We picked up my birds and headed for headquarters, arriving just about the time my host came after me. His trip to town had been successful. He had closed a deal, and I had again learned something from Joe Terry.

# 5 | The Quail Call

The next time you go quail hunting and you have your gun and ammunition packed and ready to go, do not forget your quail call! It is one of the important adjuncts of your quail shooting equipment.

The first one I ran into was many years ago, a large cumbersome piece, but it worked! Later one came out made by a Mr. Hodges of Springville, California. It was quite workable and easier to carry, but it was made of pine and absorbed moisture. Later, Neil Barton, an old quail hunter, who was quite proficient in making fishing rods, tackled the job and made them out of dead manzanita. He made hundreds of them and sold them easily. When Mr. Barton passed away, Millard Kibbe, the advertising man of Visalia, had them made in Mexico of Mexican mahogany. They also were very good. I still have some of them.

Let me tell you how I became proficient with a quail call. Years ago, and for quite some time. the Visalia Sportsman's Association raised quail with bantams on Northeast Third Avenue of this city. There were always some birds there, kept for the eggs. I would go to the pens in the late afternoon, sit on a box and talk to them by the hour. Many times I would become so interested learning their "lingo" I would be late for dinner.

After I became proficient, we never went quail hunting without a call. In those days we hunted the muscat vineyards of the valley in the vicinity of Kingsburg and the area around Sultana, Orosi, Cutler and Yettem. We would drive along the roads, stop occasionally and call. If someone got an answer, we would get permission from the owner and the hunt was on. When we went to the hills, it was the same procedure.

There is one thing that you must do when you get out of your car, you must be quiet when you make your call. Birds will not answer if there is any noise; remember, quiet!

My quail hunting partner, Burrel Hyde, and I used to use this procedure for years and always with good luck. We knew right where the birds were. Twice in my experience, I said just the right thing with my call. The first time I was hunting with R. J. Chatten near the Lucerne vineyard, north and west of Hanford. We stopped our car and I called and the birds answered. Chatten went in to headquarters to get permission and I sat down on the curb and used my call. So help me, they came from all directions. When Chatten returned I had the whole covey of some 150 birds around me and within 75 yards and in a muscat vineyard! When the birds flushed, we shot into the air to scare them. They went to cover, and we went to work with two staunch pointers and a couple of guns. It was a great morning.

On the other occasion, Jim Fluty, Visalia chief of police, came by the office with, "Buck, it is a beautiful day. Let's go bird hunting." I could not think of a reason not to go, so we headed for home to change our clothes and pick up our dogs and decided to go to the Blain field on the Gill ranch. We got there about 10:30, cast the dogs off, found the birds and had them in a ravine fully covered. I do not recall how long it took us, but I do remember that they were mostly pointed birds and flying uphill. There we were, all through. We had finished and had nothing to do.

I had noticed a mountain road going north over the mountain. I asked Fluty if he knew where it went. He said, "No." So I answered, "Let's find out." We loaded up and started to climb and wound up in a flat on top of a hill, which I

# The Quail Call

recognized as the old Wiley Hinds homestead where I had hunted with my father 40 years before. We had our lunch and sat down on a rock to rest. I took out my quail call and started to call. They started to come from all directions and in quantities. We sat perfectly still with birds all around us but already with our limits! I have often thought of those two occasions. I wish I knew what I said with that quail call.

*Mike on point -- the real thrill of quail shooting.*

# 6 | Quail Hunting, For Sportsmen Only

by
Ian I. McMillan,
Shandon, California
California's outstanding authority
on California Quail

(Mr. McMillan was asked to add a chapter to this book and supplied the following.)

Quail hunting was once a highly developed art in the sagebrush country of Central and Southern California. This was true also of the mixed woodlands in the foothills along the eastern border of the Great Central Valley. In recent decades, however, the big coveys that previously supported a thriving market-hunting trade and offered opportunity for the full development of the arts and crafts of quail hunting, have generally disappeared or remain only in remnant proportions.

With the decline of the resource, many of the older and more experienced quail hunters have left the field. Their hunting arts and skills, that evolve only through on-the-ground experience and direct cultural transmission, have faded out along with the big coveys. Consequently, a new generation of sportsmen has grown up, eager to hunt quail but without training or discipline in the ethics and rules that must be practiced if the real values of

## Quail Hunting, For Sportsmen Only

quail hunting are to be realized and if the hunting resource is to be preserved.

A bag of game to take home for the table is certainly an essential objective and most fitting conclusion to a successful hunt. However, to fully enjoy and appreciate quail hunting, it is necessary that birds bagged be regarded as of secondary importance to the hunting. The manner in which the game is taken must be of primary importance in determining the success of the hunt.

Regardless of these requirements, far too many hunters regard "the limit" as the sole objective of their hunting and make no distinction between clean wing shooting and ground-sluicing "pot-shots." This type of hunting by excessive numbers of hunters that now crowd the coverts each fall wherever hunting is allowed on either public or private quail range, can only have adverse effects on all quail hunting. Not only does the game resource suffer misuse and depletion, the real values of quail hunting are also lost, and the image of the true quail hunter is sadly tarnished.

Hopefully, on some private lands where quail are still maintained in good numbers, hunting practices are carefully conducted to assure optimum recreational value without damage or depletion of the game resource. Generally these programs work by simply establishing and following those simple rules of sportsmanship which have traditionally governed the ways in which quail should be brought to bag.

To comply with these rules, with the main emphasis on the hunting, as distinguished from the amount of game taken, a trained bird dog is almost essential. There is a popular expression among quail hunters that "quail hunting without a dog is like dancing without music." It is true that some expert quail hunters do not use dogs and that many dogs taken into the field are useless. However, it is generally agreed that quail should not be hunted without a dog. They will at least retrieve.

lost or crippled birds, and to fully enjoy the sport it is necessary to use dogs of the pointing breeds. Setters and pointers, when properly trained, are excellent retrievers, and to see an eager bird dog while racing at full speed suddenly scent game and slide into a keen, staunch point is a sight to be remembered long after the shooting is forgotten.

Assuming that such dogs are to be used, their main role in the hunt is to locate game. In areas of extensive cover and rough terrain, it is sometimes very difficult to find the winter coveys, even where there is an abundant population. After the first fall rains, California quail are able to get along without water and are able to range more widely and occupy areas remote from where they are found earlier in the dry season. Hawks that prey on quail are more common in fall and winter and their activities tend to make the coveys seek the safest refuge and to be more quiet and furtive than at other times of the year. In quail season, during November, December and January, the most enthusiastic and wide-ranging sportsman may complete what he thinks is a thorough search and find no birds, where an experienced bird dog would have no trouble finding coveys.

At the beginning of a hunt a good quail dog ranges freely and indicates when birds are scented. This gives the sportsman an opportunity to maneuver the birds into whatever position he thinks will make the best hunting. After the strategy of the hunt is decided upon, the quail are flushed and the course of their flight marked. It is best to withhold shooting at this first rise. The excitement and confusion that commonly occurs when a covey is bombarded on the first rise may cause the best bird dog to get out of control and develop bad habits. Such shooting is usually wild and haphazard and results in the crippling of birds; it also interferes with accurate observation of the covey's flight.

After the birds are flushed and relocated the real sport begins. California quail, while strong and fast on the wing, are not

# Quail Hunting, For Sportsmen Only

capable of sustained flight. They are exceptionally fast and deceptive runners, but when forced to fly and followed closely, their natural mode of escape is to scatter and hide. Each individual, or perhaps a small group, will choose a particular hiding spot where, by remaining absolutely motionless and with their protective coloration, they are safe from the inexperienced hunter as well as natural enemies. Many a sportsman, after flushing a sizable covey, has abandoned the hunt in failure and despair when he was almost stepping on quail that were hiding all around him. At this stage of the hunt, pointing bird dogs can perform at their best.

After the birds have taken cover in this manner, it is usually best to allow a few minutes for their scent to move about. In this way the dogs can locate and point them with more accuracy and the sportsman can be rested and relaxed for accurate shooting. This is the climax of the hunt and should not be hurried. Here is where all the skill and finesse of bird hunting can be brought into play.

Here is where the bird dog must be able to "do it all:" locate the hiding birds; point them accurately and staunchly; retrieve all birds dropped, including those that may be winged and able to run without handicap through dense cover. There are dogs that do all this and for those who have learned to hunt quail with them, there is no such thing as "quail hunting" without them.

In this type of hunting, where the birds burst from the short cover and are taken over a pointing dog in clean-wing shooting, the maximum in sport and recreation is realized with a minimum of loss and damage to the game population. In view of what must be done to restore and preserve the California quail and in consideration of its rare sporting qualities, it seems only proper and consistent to require the highest type of sportsmanship of those who hunt this greatest of all game birds.

*The group at San Miguel consisted of (sitting) Frank Blessing, Dick Chatten, an unidentified friend of the host; (standing) Jack Overland, Jim Fluty, Cy Parkin, Buck Buckman, and an unidentified friend of the host.*

# 7 | On the San Miguel

A few Republicans are living who remember Alf Landon's try for the Presidency, and I am one of them. I also remember a quail shoot in that year. Ike Glass, a special agent for the Nevada Fire Insurance Company and an ardent quail hunter, had made arrangements for our group of quail shooters in this area, consisting of Cy Parkin, Dick Chatten, Frank Blessing, Jim Fluty and myself, to meet him in Paso Robles, at the hotel where we were to headquarter with guns, dogs and ammunition as well as a deck of cards and some change. There were five of us and six good gun dogs in our party and three men and four dogs with Glass. All did not play poker, so we had the right size game for the evening and were ready for the next morning's shoot bright and early, after a good breakfast.

Ike had arranged for the shooting privilege with the landowners on each side of the San Miguel River, some nine miles north of Paso Robles on property now occupied by Camp Roberts, the Nacimiento and the San Antonio Reservoirs, which did not exist at that time. At intervals on the San Miguel were flatlands of 30 to 80 acres, covered with wild rose bushes. It was a quail paradise. They were everywhere and by the hundreds in great coveys.

We were there about 8 a.m. We checked in at the landowners home, so he would know who was on the property, and drove down the river to the first of the level areas. We cast off dogs with us following in line when, so help me, a covey of some 500 birds flushed and we shot to scare them. They went to cover in the rose bushes and I saw nine dogs on point at one time. It is difficult even to imagine such a sight, but we actually saw it several times! It was beautiful! From the dog's standpoint it was wonderful, but there were just too many shooters, so after a few moments we held a council of war and divided up into groups of three, after which we hunted in different directions. It made little difference to the individual shooter, because there were birds everywhere.

I understand that you can still hunt on Camp Roberts, by permission, but of course, times have changed. There are perhaps 20 shooters now where there was only one in those days and the laws were neither enforced nor obeyed as they are today.

Later on we learned an interesting fact about shooting in this area. We returned after the first rains and there were few birds along the lowlands. They had moved up into the oak timber with the large bunches of moss hanging all over them. We had few birds and they were hard to flush out of the trees and we, of course, had no dog work. This was a disappointment to me. I don't think I would go quail hunting without a dog. I never have and I am too old to start. A good dog makes the hunt.

Ike Glass, Dick Chatten and I, with our three good dogs, went down the river to the last ranch. We had previously checked in with the owner. We again cast the dogs off to find some birds, and it was not many moments thereafter that Dick yelled "Point," so we closed in and flushed a covey of some 200 which went up the hill to the right. Ike said, "Let them go, we will be in another covey soon," and we were. We went through an open gate when we flushed another covey of some 100 or more and they acted much better, flying down to the river to another flat place covered with rose bushes. We followed the dogs and soon had three dogs on point.

At this point, a car drove up and a young man jumped out with "Good morning, men, do you know where you are hunting?" We answered with another "Good morning," and "Yes, we do, we have permission," and we named the landowner. He asked, "Did you come through that open gate?" The answer, of course, was "Yes." He smiled and said, "Well, the gate should not be open. You are on the Hearst Ranch."

We, of course, were taken aback. I then noticed that he had an advertisement with a picture of Alf Landon on the side of his automobile. I asked him, "You said we are on the ranch of William Randolph Hearst?" He said, "Yes." When I asked him what he was doing with a picture of Alf Landon on the side of his car, he smiled and said, "Mr. Hearst never tells his employees who to vote for." He then, very politely, said, "Gentlemen, see that road? I am going up that road west and I am not coming back." He climbed in his car and left. He could not tell us that we could finish our hunt, but he did it in another way and like a gentleman.

It did not take long to get our limits, which we did. We then went through the open gate into the land where we had permission, divided our birds with the landowner and departed for Paso Robles to await the next day's shoot, which was a repetition of the first day's hunt, but perhaps a little better than the first from a dog's standpoint. We had better dog work, and I enjoyed it more.

They tell me there is still good hunting on the San Miguel, but, of course, they do not have as many birds. It is hunted to a greater extent. They have no way of controlling the shooting.

It was a great outing with a lot of real dog work. I enjoyed seeing the nine dogs on point at one time which, incidentally, can only happen with plenty of birds. We thanked Ike Glass for the shoot. He and his friends headed north for San Francisco, and we headed east for Tulare County.

# 8 | Mountain Quail

This fine bird, the largest of our quail, is found in most of our western states. I have hunted it in Idaho, Oregon and California as far south as Caliente in Kern County. It is a beautiful bird of reddish blue with spotted underbreast and a plume, or topknot, that sticks right out of its forehead some 2½ inches long. It weighs approximately 12 ounces, about twice the size of our California valley quail and the Bobwhite of the South.

Our California quail has the reputation of being a runner. It cannot hold a candle to the mountain variety. I do not remember many occasions when I have had a good piece of dog work while hunting them. One time when on a hunt in Kern County with Mr. Vincent Clerou of Bakersfield, a sporting goods dealer who knows that country like a book, and my old shooting partner, Burrel Hyde of Visalia, my fine pointer Rex came to a staunch point. I yelled to Hyde to take the shot, thinking it was on California quail, because that was what we were hunting at the time. He walked into the flush and three mountain quail came out. Hyde made a double and I grassed the third as it came by me, and that was all. Clerou said that the others had run away from us way up the hill! We finished with the birds we were hunting, but the mountain variety gave us the go-around.

While the two varieties overlap to some extent, I have seen the mountain quail at an elevation of some 7,000 feet and have watched them in late fall of the year run, in single file, for the lower elevations. If there is a snow storm coming, this bird will

# Mountain Quail

move out, while our California quail will stay in its own habitat, sometimes starving.

I remember one time, while fishing for trout on the middle fork of the Kaweah River, in an area we know as River Valley, I was sitting on a log, waiting for my fishing partner and taking a rest when a mother mountain quail, with perhaps a dozen little birds about half grown, settled on the same log with me, absolutely unafraid. I never moved, but they paid no attention to me and they were within 10 feet, without fear. I enjoyed the visit.

Mountain quail were very plentiful in the early 1920's, especially in the Shaver Lake area of Fresno County. There is a plateau area, between Ockenden on the Shaver Lake road and Dinkey Creek that was alive with this bird. It was mostly owned by Mr. and Mrs. Tom Ockenden, who lived on the ranch. Tom did not hunt, but did not care if we did, provided we stayed with them and played bridge, a game which was an obsession to each of them. We enjoyed the game, too, so when they asked us for a bridge game we knew that we also had a quail shoot.

I recall one occasion at the height of the mountain quail population when Tom Ockenden invited us for a weekend visit to play bridge. He also invited Mr. and Mrs. Paul Eldred, a quail-shooting friend of mine from Fresno. We loaded up my small English setter Peggy and my 28 gauge Parker Brothers, picked up our friends and headed for Ockenden's. After the dog was bedded down, we had dinner and the game was on. They had invited another couple, and the stakes were 1-50th of a cent. (Mrs. Ockenden did not believe in gambling.) Well, the sun was up when we quit. We had breakfast, and Eldred and I shouldered our guns, took Peggy and went quail hunting.

We had not gone a quarter of a mile when he had them all around us. There were quail everywhere. It took less than an hour for each of us to get our limit of 10, and what a beautiful string of birds it was! On returning to the house we dressed our birds and went to bed, with no bridge until after dark.

On the second evening, we kept Tom Ockenden busy again but stopped at midnight and hit the hay. We wanted a good shoot for at least one day. We were in birds within 15 minutes after leaving the house the next morning. They were in the low buck brush, and almost all of our dead birds fell right in the middle of a big bunch of deer brush. If we had not had a wonderful retriever like Peggy we would have come out with but few birds. It was just great to see that little setter dive in, wiggle around, whine some, but come out with her big bird. We had a fine shoot but little dog work except in retrieving. They are not a bird for dogs but, for sportsmen without a dog, they make a wonderful sport and should not be overlooked.

The birds reached an all-time low for several years but have made a comeback in California and are again hunted. Try them, and you will be surprised.

# 9 | Bobwhite Quail

I had read so much about the wonderful hunting provided by the bobwhite quail of the South, I had made up my mind that if I ever had an invitation or an opportunity, I was going to take advantage of it.

Late in the fall of 1948, we were called on by a young special agent of one of the insurance companies whom we represent and he, too, was a bird shooter, having been raised in Pontotoc, Mississippi, the heart of bobwhite quail in that state.

During our conversation, he said that his father could arrange a shoot for me and it was not many days before I had an invitation from his father, who had been a bird shooter and who had retired from the sport. He was a practicing attorney in Pontotoc.

It did not take me long to persuade Mrs. Buckman to accompany me on a trip back to the Deep South with the understanding that I would not shoot on too many days of the total spent while visiting Dixie again.

On a leisurely trip across the states on Highway 66 we reached Jackson, Mississippi, then drove north to Tupelo and a few miles west to Pontotoc, where we were to try our first experience with bobwhite. We found our host, a wonderful southern gentleman, in his office. After a most enjoyable visit, he directed me to my guide for the next day. I had no trouble locating him, and while we were discussing our shoot it started to rain. Harry DeKay, my partner for the shoot, said, "I do not like this." It was dark and pouring rain. I asked him, "Why? We would like to have some of it in California."

That evening we found out a tornado had hit some miles east near Tupelo and had killed 14 people. Harry knew his weather. The next day we were to find out what he knew about bobwhite quail.

I met him the next day about 9 o'clock. We picked up his dog and started for the country. We could not drive far because of the wet road, so we parked our car and took to the fields. I did not take long to find out that he knew bobwhite hunting and that he had been an employee of the Mississippi Fish and Game Department. We had not gone very far when his dog froze stiff as a poker. We walked in and a covey of some 20 birds flushed. Harry made a double and I found out that one would do no good shooting into a covey. But I did connect with my second shot on a single which flew to my right. I found out that one should pick out an individual bird and not just shoot into the covey.

This was all new to me. We have a California bird which seldom gives one a covey shot. Our quail shooting is mostly on singles after the main covey has flushed. In Mississippi and in other Southern states, they seldom go after the singles. It is mostly covey shooting. It was a revelation to watch DeKay work. He knew pretty well where he would find the birds. He knew his country. We were not after numbers. We wanted a few to have for dinner that evening and had no trouble in getting them.

I was surprised to find that they seemed smaller than our California bird, which weighs about six ounces. We weighed some and found that they averaged about 5½ ounces. This, he said, was caused by the importation and planting of some Mexican bobwhite in the years before. He said that they are a much smaller bird.

I also found that they would take to the timber when flushed and that was different and difficult close shooting. We tried a covey in thick timber and discovered my 28 gauge Parker just the gun for birds in Mississippi underbrush and timber. DeKay could not understand it, but it worked. It was light and easy to handle. He was using a 12 gauge, which was fine when the birds were in the open.

At about 2 o'clock, we figured we had enough birds for the dinner we had been invited to at the beautiful Southern antebellum home of Mr. and Mrs. Fontaine. We returned to town, cleaned our birds, and I had finished my first bobwhite shoot. I had come to the conclusion, and from an expert, that bobwhite are perhaps better birds for dog work on the full covey. I found that their coveys are seldom over 20 birds, while our California quail may be a couple of hundred. Our birds seldom hold as a covey. Only on occasion can a dog handle them for a shot. The Southerners seldom go after the singles while that is where we get our dog work and shooting.

That evening we were treated to a typical Southern dinner of bobwhite quail, hominy grits and corn pone....something out of this world for a westerner. The next morning we again thanked our host and hunting guide, Harry DeKay and Mrs. Mary DeKay, and headed for our destination, Thomasville, Georgia. Reaching there we checked in at the old Hotel Thomas and decided to rest a day or so before calling J. T. Groover, with whom we had reservations for personal hunting service.

Here we were at the end of the trail, after years of hearing about the bobwhite being the ultimate for dog work in quail hunting. Being an old California quail hunter for many years, I wanted to compare them myself as to their qualities for dog work. I could not see much difference with the shooting in Mississippi and California during the short period I had been shooting the bird near Pontotoc in Mississippi.

We called Mr. Groover the next day and he came in to make arrangements for our hunt the following day. He came the next morning by automobile and took me to Boston, Georgia, where I was transferred to the traditional Georgia quail hunting wagon, it being what we in the West call a two-seated buckboard. I had two mules and two boxes with two bird dogs in each and a black man to handle the dogs, as well as a sharecropper to drive the team.

My reaction was that it was a deluxe method of hunting quail. In fact, it was almost a lazy man's way, after 40 or 50 years of walking for our bird in the West.

After a short drive, we were in quail country and it was not long before the dog handler called, "Point." We drove to him and I had to step out of the buckboard to get a shot. This I did and made the shot on a single to my right. There were but a few birds in this covey, so I refrained from shooting my second shot. This was repeated three times before lunch, with but few birds in each covey. Our shots were all covey shots. We had no single ones because the birds went into the timber, and we did not follow them. After lunch we found two additional small coveys before we decided we had had enough. We called it a day and went to headquarters.

They told me that at one time the birds went to cover in the short sedge but that the last few years the birds had changed their habits and that now they head for the "tall and uncut" and that the hunters seldom followed them. While the shooting was mostly covey shooting, the dog work was intense and solid.

One must remember that our birds, after hatching and when nearly grown, get together with other groups and form another, greater covey. Some I have seen are mentioned in this book with as many as 2,000 birds, while the bobwhite, after hatching, form a new covey of their own and one seldom sees a covey of over 20 birds. For that reason I am inclined to believe that we get more shots over a point shooting our California quail than shooting bobwhite, if you know how to make the western bird go to cover. My method of doing this is to make a lot of noise when the covey is first flushed, shooting into the air and yelling. Sometimes this takes a second or third flush, but

## Bobwhite Quail

when you get them to cover you will have a field day with a good staunch bird dog.

After a couple of days shooting from a Georgia hunting wagon I was invited for a bird hunt by the proprietor of the Hotel Thomas, who was a bird shooter himself and to say that we enjoyed it would be putting it mildly. I had a great afternoon. We found four coveys with his two wonderful staunch setters, but no single shooting. It seems that one does not get too much single shooting in that area.

After a day's rest I found a bird shooting guide by the name of Caps who had the reputation for wonderful, well trained, staunch bird dogs who hunted very close to the walking quail shooter. I wanted to again try walking them up, as I had done in Mississippi. I hunted by this method for three days, and so help me, I could not see any perceptible difference. It was mostly covey shooting. That was fine and enjoyable hunting, but with all due respect to the man who has always shot the bobwhite, I personally like the shooting of California quail over a good bird dog. One does not find as many coveys but he has many, many more birds, singles and doubles.

*Sport retrieving five birds. The finest bird dog I ever owned. He wanted to do what you wanted him to do.*

# 10 | I Learn About Quail

By Charley Dickey
Reprinted from *Outdoor Life*: Copyright © 1963
Popular Science Publishing Co., Inc.

(Mr. Buckman has obtained permission of *Outdoor Life* and the author, Charley Dickey, for the reprinting of the following article which appeared in the well known magazine in 1963.)

There are several cardinal rules a hunter must never break if he expects to get repeat invitations from landowners. Buck had just shattered the whole book of hunting etiquette by insulting our host's sister-in-law. I was hastily plotting the best way to sneak off the ranch before we got kicked off, leaving behind some of the best California (valley) quail hunting in the west.

C. T. Buckman, an insurance broker from Visalia, California, has been hunting for most of his 72 years. As the result of an automobile accident, he uses a cane, and I knew he could not move as fast as I hoped to scamper, but after all, he'd started the trouble.

We were hunting on the Ike McMillan ranch near Shandon, California, nestled in the Coast Range of San Luis Obispo County. Ike runs a flock of 1,200 valley quail along with cows and barley on his 1,300-acre ranch in the hills. He was on the floor of a shallow canyon with a setter and pointer. Buck and I stood on the rim 75 yards away as he flushed quail from a broken covey toward us for tricky pass-shooting. Alta McMillan, wife of Ike's brother Don, was backing us 25 yards farther up the canyon and was consistently knocking down quail at 40 and 50 yards with her full-choke Remington 12 gauge Sportsman. Buck finally lowered his 28 gauge Parker double and stood by to watch the shooting exhibition.

When Alta centered her seventh quail, Buck couldn't stand it any longer. "She's the shootingest blank blank I ever saw!" he said.

I agreed, but Buck was too earthy in his choice of words and had spoken too loudly. Alta stiffened. Then she turned and walked toward us rapidly with long determined strides.

"Uh, oh. I've done it now," whispered Buck.

There was nothing for us to do but wait. She charged up to Buck, looked him straight in the eyes, and said, "Thanks! That's the nicest compliment a hunter ever paid me. I'm honored to be a member of the shooting Sons of Brotherhood."

Buck and I sagged in relief. She smiled, walked over to her stand, and blasted a distant quail to finish out her limit of what was then (1962-63) eight California quail. Limit for 1963-64, however, has been boosted to 10 birds a day, and, throughout most of the state, the season runs November 2 through January 1.

In a few minutes we saw Ike coming over the canyon rim toward us, his dogs at heel. I thought back to the time I'd first met him. Sportsmen all over California had told me, "If you want to learn anything about quail, you should see I. I. McMillan at Shandon."

Between 1936 and 1946, Ike saw exactly one pair of quail on his ranch. Changing farming conditions, the loss of escape cover, dry weather, and other factors had depleted the quail on his ranch and much of the surrounding area. He decided to do something about it, and he was the driving force behind the organization of the Cholame Township Sportsmen's Association which won the 20th *Outdoor Life* Conservation Award (see "Charter for Cholame," *Outdoor Life*, December, 1954).

A keen observer and an ardent student of wildlife, Ike realized there were many obstacles to bringing the quail back, even in a land where they had once flourished. He analyzed the

Ian I. McMillan testing a quail guzzler on his private shooting ground.

situation carefully and began planting food and cover. In this area, the farmers are lucky to get 10 inches of rain a year, and Ike knew he had to provide a permanent water supply. He built small, refillable guzzlers, modified after a permanent type pioneered by Ben Glading of California's Department of Fish and Game.

In 1946, Ike released 12 pairs of pen-reared California quail, some survived, and by 1952 he had an estimated 750 birds. It was not as easy as it sounds. He planted a variety of cover but not all of it caught. He experimented with different types of guzzlers. He learned not to feed his quail artificially except when feed was scarce in the winter or located too far from protective cover; Ike wanted strong birds capable of foraging for themselves. He developed nesting cover, and his water supply was scattered so that mated pairs could get their young to water soon after hatching. For a short time he feuded with predators but soon discovered that the best predator control was to provide his coveys with a variety of escape cover.

California quail roost in trees, often as many as 300 or more in a single tree. As his quail population expanded, Ike discovered that he was short of good roosting trees. He made a great contribution to quail management when he designed and built artificial roosts. They were designed so that ground predators could not climb up the supporting poles, which held a framework of 2x4's on which he made a platform of piled branches. The branches were arranged loosely enough for quail to work inside of but not open enough for owls or hawks to follow. The quail gratefully took to the artificial roosts at once, and Ike has counted as many as 400 birds in a roost from flash pictures he made at night.

By 1956, Ike had a wintering population of 1,000 quail. He found that quail brush was best suited for his ranch and continues to develop it. As he studies the quail each day, he makes modifications in habitat to keep the population high. He

## I Learn About Quail

frequently shakes up the roosts to keep the branches from becoming compacted and hindering the quail.

As I drove into Ike's ranch on a hot July day, I was immediately impressed with the variety of cover surrounding his home. There were scores of quail ducking in and out of the brush. I parked in the driveway and then noticed a pickup truck with a young setter in the back watching the quail. Suddenly I realized the dog was not tied. I sat in the car for 10 minutes as quail darted back and forth. The setter paced the truck bed, never missing a bird, but he made no sign that he intended to jump out.

Finally I went up to the house and knocked. Though I had not met Ike before, the first words I said were, "How in the world does that setter stay in the truck with that swarm of birds, running around him?"

Ike's tanned face did not change expression from the stern look he'd given me when he opened the door. "Because I told him to," he said.

Then and there I knew I'd found a bird-dog man. Later, as he gave me his de luxe tour of the ranch, he remarked that hunting quail without a dog was like dancing without music.

Now, on that November afternoon when Ike walked toward Buck and me, he asked, "How many have you down?"

"Twelve altogether," said Buck. "I've got four in the canyon, and Alta has eight on the other side."

I wondered why Ike had not stayed in the canyon to make his dog handling easier, but I had forgotten that he is a purposeful man. It quickly developed that Ike wanted to put on a show with Sport, a five-year-old pointer, and Tex, a setter of two.

With brisk commands and hand signals, Ike sent the dogs down the canyon walls. Tex was faster and came back with the first quail, but Sport brought in two. I watched in amazement as the dogs ran up and down the steep walls until they had all 12 quail. Sport came in with a pair each time. Perhaps his greater experience had taught him doubles mean less work.

I was long and lavish in my praise, as Ike handled the dogs more like Australian sheep dogs than retrievers. Buck laughed. "You haven't seen anything yet," he said. "Sport will bring in five at a time."

I ignored the remark as a typical hunter tale, and we climbed in Ike's truck, took Alta to the ranch house, and headed for another covey. We drove through barley stubble to another area that had been developed in feed and cover. Ike got out his Winchester Model 12 and I loaded my Remington 58 with three 20 gauge shells. I should mention that Buck had fired only four shells to get his four birds; with his open barrels he could not take the long shots Alta had.

The dogs sat by the truck waiting anxiously until Ike shouted, "Hiuuh!" They sprinted across the low lying cover and began working the rows of quail brush. I saw Tex's tail speed up, and he suddenly crouched into a tense point. Sport running wide open, saw him and skidded into an honor 20 yards away.

The three of us came in slowly from behind the dogs. We kept an even line with Ike in the center, Buck on the right, and I took the left flank. As we passed Tex, a covey exploded and fanned out. I rushed my first shot and missed but caught a curving cock bird with the second shot and saw it go down. My third shell was wasted, and I turned to ask what the others had bagged. Ike had two down and Buck had dropped two close by.

Ike called Tex in and put him at heel. "Buck, I guess we'll have to prove to Charley that Sport will retrieve five birds at one time," he said. He gave it time to soak in and then asked me, "Where did your bird fall?"

"He hit over by that little clump of quail brush," I said, pointing.

## I Learn About Quail

Ike sent Sport over, and the eager pointer quickly found the bird and started in. Ike shouted, "Whoa!" and Sport stopped instantly. Then Ike sent him toward the other birds. Still carrying the first one, Sport soon found two more and picked them up. He wanted to bring them in but Ike kept holding him out. Sport shuttled around until he located the fourth bird, but when he grabbed it another quail slipped out of his mouth. Ike said nothing and we watched as Sport finally worked all four birds between his jaws. In a few seconds he found the fifth bird. He tried to pick it up but lost two. Ike stood watching intensely and encouraging the dog with, "Get 'em all!"

Sport kept juggling the birds until he had all five. I looked over at Buck's blue eyes, and they were twinkling with delight. Sport came trotting in with his overload, stopped at Ike's feet, and sat patiently waiting for Ike to take them. There was hardly a ruffled feather on any of the five quail.

I was speechless. Though records are not kept on retrieving, I was sure I had just seen a sort of world record.

"Too bad you didn't have your camera," said Buck.

"Don't worry," I replied. "We'll try to set it up in the open where there's no brush in the way and shoot it in sequence. No one will ever believe this story unless I have the pictures to prove it." (Later, at Ike's house, Sport repeated his field performance twice for the camera -- once for color and once for black and white.)

"There were only about 20 birds in that rise," said Ike. "The covey must be split. Let's hit that next strip of brush and find 80 or 90 quail that are missing."

I was reared in the South on bobwhite, and I cannot get used to the large coveys of California quail, especially in dry years when the birds concentrate in vast numbers around waterholes. In much of California, a covey of 100 birds is routine. I have seen many coveys with over 200 birds in them, and Ike has one covey that has 400-600 birds in the winter.

Points -- Sport and Tex each on point and the author trying to reach them at the McMillan Ranch.

# I Learn About Quail

It is generally difficult to get a covey shot on large concentrations of California quail. If there is good grassy cover the birds may hold as a unit, but where the ground cover is sparse, the quail run and run, darting from covey to brushy cover. As long as the covey stays intact, it is extremely hard for the dogs to point them or the hunters to catch up. It is not unusual to follow a running covey for a mile and never get a shot.

In most cover situations, the trick in hunting California quail is to break up the covey. Once they are flushed and scattered, they will hold unbelievably tight for dog work. Their gray color blends in perfectly with the ground and vegetation, and they can hide on ground that is almost bare. Often I have passed patches of cover no larger than a frying pan and had two or three birds burst out behind me.

In November and December, the open season for quail in California, some of the best hunting areas may not have had rain for six or eight months. Scenting condition, except in early morning or late afternoon, will test any pointing dog. It takes top dog work to find singles in dusty cover, and sometimes the hunter will flush birds dogs have not pointed. Scattered singles, or groups of four or five, often hold tighter than bobwhite quail. I have seen California quail land in an isolated clump no larger than a washtub and had the dogs go on point. I have walked up, kicked the brush four or five times, stomped on it, turned around to pull the dogs off, and then had the quail scoot out behind me.

One trick frequently used to break a running covey is to shoot over it as soon as possible. On occasions when this has not worked for me, I have sometimes welcomed wild-running dogs that would overtake and scatter the birds. Where a covey has been well broken, and I'm fairly sure the quail are holding, I may wait five or 10 minutes before going after them with the dogs. In dry weather, this helps the dog work, as the birds have time to give off more scent.

*"Bev" Thompson, a prominent attorney of Fort Worth, Texas, and the author hunting on the McMillan Ranch, Shandon, California; Sport on point with Tex backing.*

When a covey is scattered, I have found it best to hold the dogs in close and work slowly. I try to kick each clump and patch of grass, even if the dogs have been by it. Often I have worked back over an area a second time and flushed more birds than on the first pass. Sometimes a third swing will flush more crafty singles. At Ike's, I saw five birds flush out of a tumbleweed that was lying on plowed, open land.

The California quail is found from the Mexican border to the Oregon line in this state, and from sea level to 5,000 feet or more. In intensely agricultural land, however, such as the San Joaquin or Sacramento Valleys, modern farming has not left

# I Learn About Quail

sufficient habitat for the quail except in isolated instances. But in the foothills of the two main mountain ranges, the Sierra and the Coastal, there are a lot of cattle, and what farming there is there has left food, cover, water, and roosting trees.

The sportsman looking for a place to hunt would do well to hit the back roads in the foothills and seek permission from landowners. Getting this may involve a lot of pre-season scouting, and because of this problem of public access to private property I believe the California quail is underharvested in many areas. However, it's been my experience that ranchers will permit quail hunting on their lands sooner than they'll allow pheasant or waterfowl hunting. If the would-be shooter has no luck with landowners, he should probe the vast state or federal holdings in the foothill country. He can find out about these from the state's Department of Fish and Game, 722 Capitol Avenue, Sacramento, California.

As Tex and Sport moved ahead of us, the main covey Ike was seeking flushed wild. We were in luck, as the 70 or 80 birds fanned out and landed in singles and small groups in good ground cover. We knew they would stick. Ike unloaded his gun and told Buck and me to handle the shooting.

Ike does a lot of hunting on his ranch and for chukars in the Temblor Mountains, but he seems to get just as much enjoyment from watching his guests shoot. He is a firm believer in taking the surplus quail on his ranch each year. He realizes there is limited carrying capacity even under the most favorable conditions and that it would be a waste not to take a reasonable harvest. To do this, Ike invites many local people, especially some of the older hunters, to hunt on his place each season. He also has a steady stream of relatives, friends, biologists and others who go afield with him, and, though his property is not, strictly speaking, open to the public, he accommodates all the hunters he can consistent with care of his breeding stock.

When Sport went on point, Ike told me to take it. I moved over quickly, expecting a single. When five quail came jetting out, however, I was so surprised that I balked and got off only two shots, and just one quail tumbled. Ike looked down at his boots, and I couldn't tell whether he was laughing or not. Buck was laughing openly, and I guess he could afford to -- he was six for six.

Buck took the next point and a brace zoomed out. He swung his little 28 gauge and the first bird crumpled. He quickly swung to the other bird -- and missed. Without taking a step, Buck reloaded and then moved slowly ahead. Another bird went out low and Buck nailed it. He had ended his day with eight quail in nine shots. I started to congratulate him on his outstanding shooting, but he was already apologizing for having missed one. To my amazement, he seemed considerably upset over it.

I eventually finished out my limit, but it didn't seem necessary to keep track of the shells I used. With Ike's guiding, the pointing of the dogs, Sport's remarkable retrieving, and Buck's marksmanship I had been, as they say in the South, in some real tall cotton.

On other trips with Buck to the McMillan ranch, I took along my setter Smokey. I admit it took a lot of nerve for me to cut my dog loose in the same field with Ike's, but Ike is a generous man. He said my dog backed his real well.

Sitting around the ranch with Ike, I've often talked with him about the future of quail hunting. He has done a terrific job of bringing quail back, though he had to learn a lot about how to do it the hard way -- by trial and error. "With all the information now available on the California quail, there is no reason any other rancher couldn't do the same thing I've done," he says. "But anyone starting such a project must realize there is a whole series of steps and none can be left out. The birds have to have feed, escape cover, nesting cover, water

# I Learn About Quail

and roosts. If just one of these is left out, it may be the limiting factor that holds back quail production. But what I've done can be accomplished on nearly any ranch, and without interfering with normal farming operations."

There's just one thing Ike has done that I don't like. Somehow Buck talked him into selling Sport. Maybe Buck even blackmailed him. What with his shooting ability, and now the ownership of the dog, I guess Buck will become well-nigh intolerable.

# 11 | Trapshooting

With my interest in shooting and my love for the smell of burning powder, there can be little doubt as to the reason why I wandered out to the California State Shoot held in Visalia in 1917. There was an additional interest for me. They were pitching double eagles, or twenty dollar gold pieces, at a line. The one closest to the line, or the winner, took all. I did not enter the contest, the main reason being that I did not have the twenty dollar gold piece. My memory is that Ed Garrett, president of the Oakland Iron Works, was cleaning up on the boys. He was an expert pitcher of the double eagle.

While I had hunted since early childhood, and I thought I knew how to handle a shotgun, I tried trapshooting and to my surprise I broke only nine out of the first 50 targets I shot at. To say the least, I was provoked. I was not a bad shot and knew clay pigeons must be easier to hit than live game, so I made up my mind to learn the sport. Frankly, though I tried with all my heart, it was over two years before I broke a 25 straight, and some years later when I broke 100 straight.

I happened to be an oddball when it came to trapshooting. I wanted to turn in a good score, but did not seem to have the desire to win unless I got into a tie and then a shoot-off. Then I really got the desire and wanted to win. A shoot-off was a challenge and I did not lose many times in all my many years of shooting clay birds. Frankly, I do not remember a shoot-off that I ever lost at our local club. I was beaten many times in the regular event, but if we had to shoot-off, a tie, I did not lose.

# Trapshooting

One of the secrets of trapshooting is having a gun that fits. One cannot break targets with a crooked field stock. It must be a straight stock that throws the load high because the target is gaining height very fast. The shooter is not shooting at the target, he is shooting above the target automatically.

I tried different guns over a period of several years, these guns being straight single barrel trap guns, but with which one could shoot only 16 yard singles and handicap targets. I always had a hungering for a Parker, so finally I purchased a DHE Parker Double so that I could shoot singles, handicap and doubles with the same gun, but it did not balance. The gun seemed barrel heavy for some reason. I could shoot around 93 to 94 per cent, but that would not get me anywhere in Class A.

One day, out at our club on the airport, a Dr. Anderson was admiring my Parker and wanted to try it. I said, "Of course." He took the gun and broke 24 out of 25. He had a number five Ithaca which he wanted me to try. I did and broke 25 straight. The gun felt good and had a wonderful balance. We traded guns and I have shot that gun all these years. It is still in my gun case and will be there forever.

There was one shoot-off that I lost that I must tell you about. It was in San Jose in the handicap at the California State Shoot. I finished the event with a 96 from 23 yards, which was the limit in those days. There was one more squad to finish and I was being congratulated on being the new state handicap champion. In the squad was a young man by the name of W. J. Derby of Modesto, California, shooting at 18 yards. Derby had never broken 25 straight at any yardage and they were sure that he would not do it here. This had to be done to tie. Well, Bill Derby did just that, so it was up to us to shoot it off. I was shooting at 23 yards and Derby at 18 yards. Bill broke 24 targets and I broke 23. Bill Derby was state champion that year and I was runner-up. It was one of the few shoot-offs that I failed to win.

Another shoot in which we both participated was at the Old Fisherman's Club Annual Invitational Shoot at Modesto. This was on the San Joaquin River on the Mapes ranch west of Modesto, the club's permanent home.

There was a handicap event in which the winners of each class, "A," "B," "C," and "D," had to shoot off at their respective handicap yardage. I was Class A and won the event and then had to shoot off with each of the winners of their class at his handicap yardage. I was shooting at 24 yards and broke 24 out of 25 to win the event in the shoot-off.

At the state shoot in Modesto, in the early Thirties, I got into a shoot-off with two of the finest shots in the West; namely, Ollie Fine of LeGrange, California, who has won the state championship probably more times than any one individual, and Sam Sharman of Salt Lake City, former president of the American Trapshooters Association and a member of the 1924 Olympic team. The shoot-off was on the second day 16-yard event. I happened to win over Ollie Fine by one target and Sam Sharman by two. I still own the clock which was the trophy.

For some unknown reason, I have always shot well while shooting in Modesto. There have always been some fine sportsmen following trapshooting in that area: Henry Garrison; Bill Silva, president of the California Fish and Game Commission; Ollie Fine; Jack Crane; Bill Derby and his father; to name but a few, and I am indeed sorry that I do not remember all of their names. Remember that I am now getting along in years.

I remember two other shoot-offs that I won in Modesto. One was with and against Jack Crane, a fine double shot. We tied in the double event. When we went up to shoot, I remarked to Jack, "Don't miss any, Jack. I'm not going to." I went straight and he missed but one.

On another occasion, and again during an Old Fisherman's Club Shoot, I got tied up with O. N. Ford of Del Monte, California, former vice president of the American Trapshooter's Association, and the one who organized the Pacific International Trapshooting Association. We were tied at the end of the shoot, with our totals on 16 yards, handicap and doubles, for high overall.

Someone suggested that it be shot off at double targets.

We both agreed and I was sitting in a car talking to Harry Lorenson, the high average shooter from Newman, California, when O. N. Ford came over bragging about his double gun. We were called to shoot when Lorenson said to me, "Buck, beat that guy or I will never speak to you again." I did not know that there was a little hard feeling between the two, but I did just what Harry asked me to do. I broke 48 out of 50 and O. N. Ford broke 45. He walked over sputtering about a "B" class shooter, meaning me. Modesto was a fine trapshooting city. I always enjoyed the city and the sportsmen who lived there.

Another shoot-off that I remember was at Las Vegas, Nevada. It was at the annual pow-wow of the California Indians, a trapshooting organization of dedicated sportsmen who had lost their permanent home at Del Monte. We hit a period when the wind came up and was trying to blow the area over into Arizona. The targets were blowing back over our heads. Such shooting is a challenge and I have always enjoyed the challenge. The harder they are, the better I have liked the shooting.

It was in the double event, 50 pair, and they were really flying around. I tied the great double shot, Maynard Henry of Los Angeles, an attorney, with 46 out of 50, which was pretty good double shooting on a quiet day. Henry afterwards was president of the Amateur Trapshooting Association, with its permanent home in Vandalia, Ohio. He since has passed away, but he was one of the great trapshooters of America.

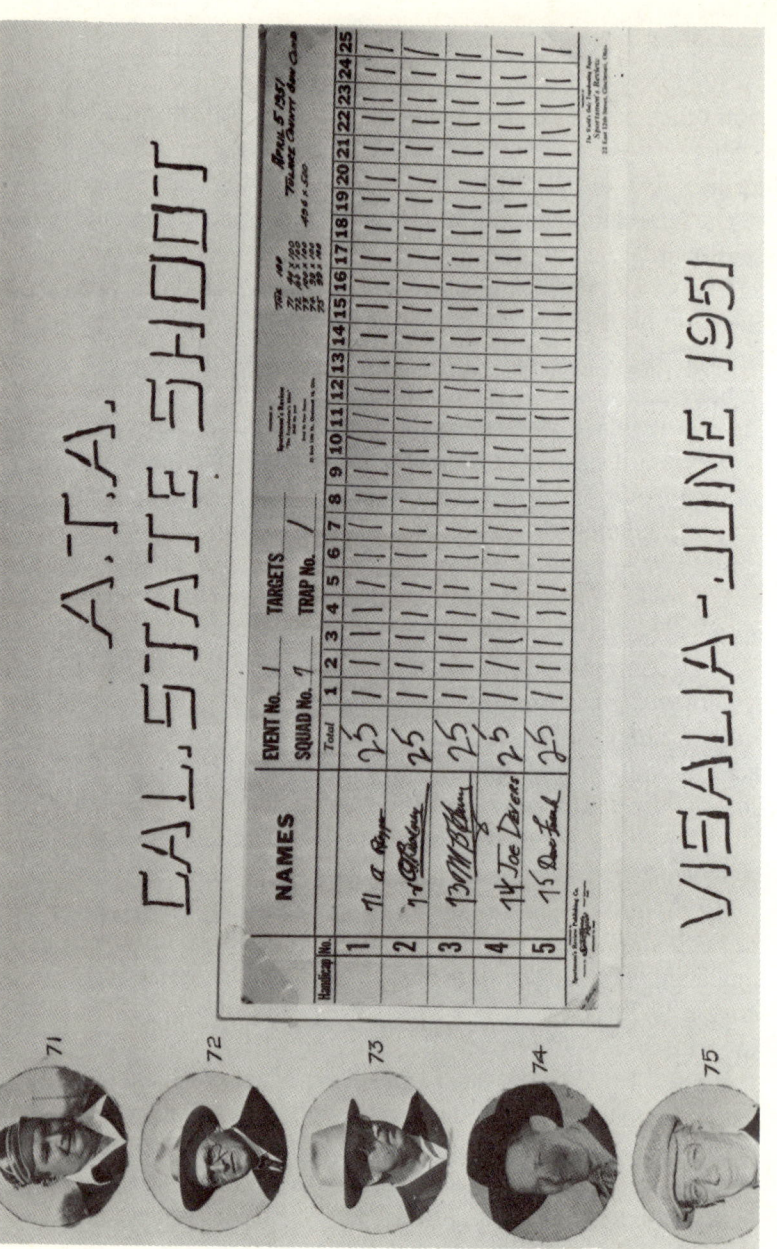

*Almost a squad world record at the time. Scores: A. Riegger, Seattle, Washington, 99; C. T. Buckman, Visalia, California, 100; M. B. Henry, Los Angeles, California, 100; Joe Devers, Reno, Nevada, 98; Dave Frank, Los Angeles, California, 99; Total*

# Trapshooting

We shot it off the same evening. The wind still was strong. Henry broke 46 out of 50 and I broke 47, I guess, because we were tied.

It was my privilege to shoot with one of the really fine squads at the state shoot in Visalia, April 5, 1951. The squad was composed of the following shooters: Arnold Riegger, the great shooter from Seattle, Washington, who led the squad; I shot the number two position and Maynard B. Henry of Los Angeles, mentioned above, was number three; Joe Deavers, the great live pigeon and trapshooter from Reno, Nevada, shot number four position, ; and Dave Frank of Los Angeles, a great trapshooter, number five. Riegger broke 99, I broke 100, Henry broke all, Joe Deavers was low man in the squad with a 98 and Dave Frank broke 99, for a squad total of 496 out of 500 targets. It was not a record at that time, but was a near record. A photo of the squad sheet of the first event at trap one is a part of this chapter. One hundred and twenty-five straight by five shooters and repeated at trap four.

I must tell you of a shoot that I lost. It was in Salt Lake City with W. J. Silva. We went to Salt Lake to take in the zone handicap. We entered the Calcutta and I was hotter than a firecracker and blowing each target into smoke. Well, I had 81 targets in the bag, dead on the scoreboard and tally sheet, when with but 19 targets to go, the rib broke loose and came back over my right shoulder and the two barrels of my double-barreled Ithaca parted and were pointed in opposite directions. There I was, with some $3,000 on the line, and I was out of the race. Let me advise you, if you want to shoot for the money seriously in trapshooting, have two guns and know where each gun shoots, because no two guns shoot exactly alike. I borrowed another gun and lost six targets out of the last 19. I would have bet most anything that this would not have happened with my own gun. I did not win what I thought was a cinch.

*1951 State Shoot winners (from left): A. Riegger, Seattle, Washington, 16 yards; M. B. Henry, Los Angeles, doubles; C. T. Buckman, preliminary handicap.*

For many years I had hoped to shoot in the Grand American Handicap at the Amateur Trap Shooting Association's permanent grounds and home at Vandalia, Ohio, and held there each August. Forrest E. Kerr, that fine sportsman and shooting companion, living on the highway between Visalia and Hanford, and I decided to go. That was in 1947, and we shot the program. It was a shooting event that I will not soon forget. There were 36 traps in a row and then eight more for practice. They had a tramway to carry the shooters from trap to trap and back to headquarters.

## Trapshooting

We hit one of those hot, humid weeks when a Californian would almost die. We would sit on the squad bench waiting for our turn to shoot and would be wet with perspiration. It was no fun. They tell me that it was not that way every year, but I never tried it again.

We happened to be squadded with Charles A. Young, the first shooter to break 100 targets from the 23-yard line in the Grand American Handicap. It had been accomplished one time before, but from the 19-yard line.

This was in the first 100 of the 16-yard targets. They would put your name up on the large bulletin board if you broke 99 or 100. I was the first to break 99 that day and got my name on the bulletin board. Before the day was over there were a dozen hundreds. And, why not there? There were over 1,800 shooters participating from all over the United States, Canada, and foreign countries. If you are a trapshooter, or ever become one, by all means take in the Grand American Handicap. The "cream of the crop" attend this shoot. The best are there, and you will get a thrill you will never forget.

It has been my pleasure to shoot with some of the best shooters in the United States; men such as Frank Troeh of Portland, Oregon, who was won more national championships than any other trapshooter; Sam Sharmon of Salt Lake City, the Olympic trapshooter and past president of the Amateur Trapshooting Association; Joe Cotant of Idaho, high average shooter; Cal Ray of Oregon; O. N. Ford of Del Monte; Phil Miller, who managed Harold's Club at Reno for several years; Al Riehl, that fine representative of Remington Arms on the coast and later Remington Arms sales chief for the United States, since retired; Leila Hall Frank, the wife of Dave Frank of Los Angeles, who shot in our championships in Visalia (Leila has probably won more championships than any other woman shooter); Helen O'Dell, that expert woman trapshooter from Le Grange, and sister-in-law of Ollie Fine; Fred and Rudy

Etchan, father-and-son team, each of whom has won many championships, and they were fine sportsmen. I have always prized these shooting friendships very highly. There were many, many others, but I do not have the space to mention all of them, for which I am indeed sorry.

In 1947 there was another shoot-off I must tell you about. It was the California State Shoot in Sacramento. On Friday, I put a 99 on the bulletin board. It was the first half of the state championship and, of course, there were not many scores ahead of it. Saturday rolled around and I was down one target when I reached my last trap. I noticed W. J. Stone of Sacramento following our squad. When I walked over and asked him how many I could miss, he said, "Oh, perhaps one," and then thought better of it and said, "No, don't miss any," and I said, "Okay, I'll get them all." And I did, going out with a 99 or 198 out of 200 for the two days. When that evening came, I found myself in a tie with Fred Dambacker, a great trap shot from Sacramento, with whom I had shot on many occasions.

In the early evening we were called to shoot it off for the championship of California. In fact, it had started to get dark. We were each introduced and as I walked out with Fred to the shooter's stand, I said, "Fred, don't miss one because I am not going to." It was now so late you could hardly see the targets, but one could see the flash of the powder as it left the barrel. When the event was over, Dambacker had lost one and I had 25 straight on the tally sheet. I had won another shoot-off, this time for championship of California.

For several years, during the late Forties and early Fifties, medals were given to the shooter who had reached the age of 65 and who had the high average for the year. The medals were a beautiful piece of craftsmanship, with a small diamond and were given by H. D. Blanchard, a large olive grower of Terra Bella and a good trapshooter. I reached the age of 65 in 1954 and was eligible to compete. I was lucky enough to finish the year with the following averages: 16 yards - .9666, handicap 24 and 25 yards - .8975, doubles - .8733. It was enough to place me first and I was presented with a medal at the next state shoot. Of this I am very proud.

At the 1969 Shoshone Indian Shoot, held at Sun Valley, Idaho, it was my privilege to enter the Shoshone Handicap where, much to my surprise, it seemed that I could not miss. I was shooting from my official handicap yardage of 23 yards, having been moved up one yard from my Amateur Trapshooting Association yardage of 24 yards and when I finished I had posted a 95.

It gave me the Shoshone handicap belt buckle of sterling silver and gold with an American silver dollar in the center. When it was presented, I remarked that I would certainly like to have a dollar minted the year of my birth, 1889. Then it would show that I won the trophy at the age of 80. The chairman of the trophy committee looked at me and said, "Buck, we will sure do it." He did, and I now have the last trophy I won while shooting targets, and it is highly prized.

Here are a few trapshooting tips:

1. Try to get squadded up with shooters of equal or better averages. They seem to carry one along.

2. Be ready to shoot when your squad is called; don't hold it up. Remember, there are others to consider.

3. When you have finished your five shots at a stand, don't start to the other position until the last man of the squad has finished and has started to make the change.

4. Concentrate. Shoot each target separately. You shoot one target 25 times in each event, not 25 targets. If you miss one, forget it. Get the next one each time until the event is over.

5. Don't hesitate to ask any dedicated trapshooter for help or advice. I've never found one who would not be glad to help in any way possible, even though he may know that you may improve and beat him.

# 12 | Setters

It has been my privilege to own a few outstanding dogs -- dogs that probably would not satisfy a field-try specialist, but close working dogs that are a pleasure to shoot over. One was a dog mostly for quail, and in our area we know about the location of the various coveys we shoot, so one does not need a far working dog to find them.

We use a quail call to good advantage and if the hunter is quiet, the birds will answer. It is always a big help to know the location of the birds. One knows better how to approach the covey after sizing up the terrain. Personally, I like a close working dog because we do not have to find the coveys, so I want the dog for pointing and making the retrieve. A close working retriever will save many a cripple and prevent its loss by getting into a rock pile.

There have been three outstanding English setters in my shooting life and some pointers, but I will try to tell you about the pointers in another chapter. The first of the setters was Peggy, a small, lovable, white, close-working, spayed bitch.

I remember that our daughter Lois was very young and would be playing jacks on the front sidewalk with Peggy down at her side. She would miss the ball and Lois would say, "Get the ball, Peggy." She would get up, retrieve it and deliver it to her at her feet. This would go on for hours, with Peggy always doing her duty.

I do not remember when I obtained this bitch, but I shot over her for many years. She was close working and staunch on point

## Setters

until something happened which I will relate later. She was a wonderful retriever, had a very tender mouth and was with you all day. We had her until she was very old, but I would not get rid of her because she had been so faithful. If I took the other dog hunting, she would sit on the porch and cry until I retrurned. I would often take her along on short hunting trips of an hour or two. If I would go for a longer trip, Mrs. Buckman would take Peggy in the front door and I would sneak out the back one.

One shoot in her later years almost ruined her, and it took a lot of work to correct the fault and again make her staunch. We were hunting on the old Giannini ranch west and north of Tulare. It was a cold, foggy day and we had the quail scattered along an old dry canal.

Peggy brought me a bird that I had failed to shoot. I started to take the bird and it flew away. Peggy sat down and looked at me with a "Well, I'll be damned!" expression on her face. This happened once or twice more. I followed her more closely in the fog, found that she was coming to point and then jumping in, trying to catch the bird herself, and once in a while she made it.

I recall one of the times we had to go to Dr. Edwards to remove a foxtail from her ear. She saw the doctor coming onto the front lawn, laid down with her head on the side and allowed him to put those tweezers into her head and remove the trouble, and then, when it was all over, she licked his hands and said "Thank you" in real dog fashion.

On another occasion, we were going to the Giannini Ranch. We went to the headquarters to get permission when Elrena, now Mrs. Fred Lagomarsino, asked us to run off anyone that might be hunting on the property. Jim Fluty, a fine bird hunter and a good shot, was with me. There was a Muscat vineyard on the west side of the house covering some 60 acres and there was a hunter and white-and-black setter on point right out in the middle. We walked out to him and recognized Emory Wilton of Tulare.

While we knew that he had hunted the property for years, I delivered the message. "We are sorry, Emory, but Elrena told us to run off any hunter we found hunting here. You have the birds all scattered and laying well. We hate to take your place; however, it is our duty."

It was hard, but I kept a straight face. Wilton did not hit the ceiling -- he hit the clouds, ZIP, BOOM, BANG! I will not repeat what he said, but you can imagine it was plenty. I could not keep my face straight and burst out laughing. Jim was with me, and Emory saw the joke. We three went to work with the three men and two dogs, Emory's setter and my Peggy. One point after another, beautiful dog work, and we were not missing many birds. If my memory is correct, we went out of there with 45 birds, a limit of 15 each.

Jim Fluty and I had a fine shoot on that property, in the vineyard mentioned and along the slough running east and west through the property. It always seemed that we could not make a dent in the quail population on the ranch. They were there by the hundreds.

For many years Dwight French, a walnut grower living on east Houston Avenue, a true sportsman and an inveterate hunter, and I make a trip to Redwood Mountain for blue grouse. The limit at that time was four and we seldom missed obtaining the limit. It was on one of these occasions that Peggy made one of her famous retrieves. I must tell you about it.

We would drive to the summit, park our car and hunt north along the top of the ridge. We almost always found plenty of birds in the area and this day was no exception. We had not gone far when a brace flushed wild. Dwight took the right bird and I the left. Both dropped dead. Peggy brought my bird to me and Dwight made his own retrieve. His dog was at home under the weather.

# Setters

We had not gone 100 yards when two got up near French and he made a double. It was nice shooting. We went over to help find the first bird, as he retrieved his own second shot. It was not long when two flushed wild and I managed to grass both of them. French and I then were even. I had not gone 50 yards when a bird got up in front of Peggy and started to the left over the canyon. I gave it the right barrel and the feathers flew. I gave it the second barrel and again the feathers flew. The bird shook itself and flew on. I watched and so did Peggy... It was out over the very bottom of the canyon when it crumpled and fell dead in the bottom of the steepest part. Peggy, in high gear, was after my number four. I could see her when she found the bird, but it was a full grown bird and she could not get it in her mouth, so she rolled it over, got the hen by the neck, and started dragging it up the hill. She dragged it for some 25 yards and then dropped it, lay down and took a rest. This was repeated several times with the same procedure.

Finally, here she was with my bird at my feet. She put it down, walked over a few feet, dropped to the ground, looked up at me with a disgruntled expression and disgusted look on her face as if to say, "Damn it, kill them dead." I wanted to give the dog a rest and French went ahead and killed his number four. We headed down the ridge to the car and for home, each agreeing that the dog work was out of the ordinary.

The next setter I owned was obtained for me by Harry Doyle, then manager of the Fire Companies Adjustment Bureau. He had him shipped from somewhere near Dallas, Texas. He was a real bird dog. The morning he came, Jim Fluty, then chief of police, and I took him out of the crate in the express office. He went to a power pole and relieved himself. After several minutes he finished, then walked over and looked at me as if to say, "Well, that is over." The setter's name was Caesar. Just where they got a name like that for a real bird dog I'll never know. It is something like the names parents sometimes give defenseless babies.

We let the dog rest for a few hours, then took him out for some exercise. We went out to the Toomey ranch where we knew there was a covey of birds and cast Caesar off. He had not run 150 yards when he stopped and froze. After a minute or two the birds ran to the east. Caesar stepped over a few feet and brought them to a halt. What covey work for a dog! Caesar knew his stuff. We watched it all from a distance. When the dog looked back at us, as if to say, "Here they are, come and get them," we could not. It was out of season. Caesar stood there like the Rock of Gibraltar. We had a fine season over that dog, but he was old and died soon after the season closed.

My next setter was Sam, from Kansas, an Englishman and a Republican. Sheriff Sandy Robinson got this dog for me. It seemed that the Democrats were trying to ship all the Republicans out of Kansas, so it would go Democratic for Roosevelt. We used Sam for one year. He, being a Republican, was tired of the way things were going and so just gave up the ghost and died after the first season. Sam was a real Republican and a fine bird dog, staunch, steady to shot and a fine retriever.

It has been my privilege to own several other setters, but none like those I have mentioned. I have tried three or four Irish Setters, but without much luck. I never owned a real Irish Setter shooting dog. The trouble was that they have bred all the shooting qualities out of them. They wanted Irish Setters for show purposes. They are a fine and beautiful dog for those who like them.

# 13 | Dove Shooting

Doves to me, and to most Upland game hunters, are among the hardest birds to bag, particularly after they have been shot at a water hole or feeding ground. They are an easy target the first day or two, and that probably is the reason so many shooters are out there opening day, after which they hang up their guns and await the opening of another season.

Personally, I do not like an opening day. There are too many shooters not caring where they shoot. The shooting is just too easy. I would much rather go out after the birds have been banged at for a few days; then they change their speed and direction almost instantly, and it is a real shoot. With a small limit it is quite easy to go straight on opening day, but after a few days one must be a real shot and must concentrate -- there can be no playing around.

Let me tell you about a shoot with Newt Young, a former supervisor of our county, a real sportsman. Newt could really handle a 20 gauge shotgun and, incidentally, a four-ounce fly rod. He was dry fly fisherman, one of the best.

We had a place at the south end of Mehrten Valley, just before we entered the Gassenberg Ranch. There were two small hills covered with small oaks. The birds came from a wheat field north of us late in the evening. We stationed ourselves some 50 yards south of the first hill, between the two, when here they came in high gear, darting and weaving from side to side directly at us and between the trees. We did not make a very good average, but it surely was sport. When we were through we had each shot up two boxes of shells. Newt had 14 birds and I had 12. It was not much of a meat shoot, but it was real sport. We shot at this location at times earlier in the afternoon when the birds came down to feed after spending the day in the oaks higher in the hills. The light was better, and so was our shooting.

Jim Fluty and I also shot this area. I saw him miss 11 straight shots with a 20 gauge and Fluty was a real shot. Let me tell you that it is the sport one is after when one goes afield, not the meat; if it were, one would go to the market. It would be much cheaper.

Forty years ago we could look for a sunflower patch or a field of dove weeds, sometimes known as turkey mullein, for a dove shoot. Today we do about the same thing with the addition of a few new grains like safflower, which they like very much when it is knocked down, and certain kinds of corn, after harvesting. Years ago we had the White Gyp Corn, but it shattered so much that farmers quit growing it. But the birds in those days would come into it by the thousands, as they now come for the harvested safflower.

I will relate a few of the dove shoots I have attended to give you an idea of what it was like. I recall the shoots held by Orval Overall, the old Chicago Cubs' pitcher, a native of Visalia, later a banker and bank manager. Orval was a good upland game shot and a fine sportsman. We hunted together on many occasions. Orval had permission to hunt on the Ward Ranch on the lower Dry Creek, north of Lemon Cove. In those days there was a lot less standing water than there is now. It did not come to the surface, so Orval would send his gardener to the Ward Ranch to dig out a hole for the water to seep into some days before the season opening. When it did open, the birds were there in the evening by the thousands. Sometimes he would have a dozen shooters from Fresno, together with his shooting friends from this area, including Burrel Hyde, Charles W.

# Dove Shooting

Berry and myself. When the birds started to come, it would sound like a state trapshoot had opened up. Imagine the birds taken out of the area in an evening! The limit was 15 and sometimes there would be 25 shooters. They usually shot the waterhole twice a week. There was no end to the birds. They just kept coming.

The same conditions existed on the Gill property on Yokohl Creek in Yokohl Valley. The water came to the surface near the fence line between the Gill Ranch and the old Lisenby Ranch. It was a dove watering place of long standing. One just cannot imagine the birds that came there to water in the old days. The shooting lasted until about 1960, when the spring dried up and the waterhole shooting ceased.

I will never forget a morning shoot with Orval Overall. He picked me up one morning early to shoot a place I had located on the Jim Tout Ranch on lower Mill Creek. The birds came into the cottonwoods and willows along the creek and they came in droves. We arrived about 7:30, and the birds were in high gear. I put my gun together and noticed Orval searching the automobile when he stopped and said, "Buck, did you hide my gun?" I had to say, "No, Orval, I haven't seen your gun." He had come dove hunting without a gun -- he had forgotten it. I seldom went hunting anywhere without two guns, so I loaned him one of mine and we had a day.

There is still some fine dove shooting in this area, but it is according to present-day standards. Frankly, we must adjust ourselves to conditions. We do not need the shooting of the birds we had 50 years ago to enjoy a day in the field with a shooting companion.

Unlike quail and pheasants, doves are hunted by three distinct methods: feeding ground, a waterhole and a flyway, with or without a dog. The hunter walks up quail or pheasant, but in dove shooting, the shooter takes a stand at a feeding ground, a waterhole or flyway and waits for the doves to come in.

Although the methods are without much effort, they are not easy if you count your shells with your results. A dove in flight seems to be a large target, this because of the wingspread and tail feathers, but its speed of flight and acrobatic antics make it a difficult target. This is particularly true in late season.

It is my opinion that doves attract more hunters inexperienced in wing shooting than any other type of bird. The ratio of empty shells to birds in the bag tell the tale. It also suggests constant pre-season practice with your shotgun for pattern, choke, conditioning and gun familiarity. Few deer hunters will go afield with a rifle that they personally had not sighted in, yet many hunters go after doves each year with shotguns they have not patterned or corrected.

Successful dove shooting demands a close, uniform pattern and a gun that points where the shooter is looking, provided he is mounting and cheeking his gun correctly.

When checking shotgun pattern, I try to duplicate actual shooting conditions, that is, as much as possible with a still target. I walk off a 40-yard range and set up a regular pattern target, or a piece of cardboard large enough to accommodate a 30-inch circle with a three-inch bull's eye in the center. Dropping back some 45 yards, I walk toward the target, eyes roving, not concentrated, then shoulder the gun and fire quickly from the 40-yard marker.

Making several targets at 40 yards, the shooter has no trouble counting the holes and figuring the percentage of holes in the circle. I quarter the circle with pencil marks to make the counting easier and to find out where and how much the concentration is; whether right or left, high or low. The average of several targets give a pretty good picrture of where the shots are striking in relation to the bull's eye.

*Waiting for the dove flight.*

It is advantageous to try all available dove loads in the various brands because some will pattern better than others in any one gun. Try both number 7½ and 8 shot, in various loads, until you find the most uniform pattern. This way may or may not be a high velocity load but will give the lighter loads a thorough testing. You may be surprised at the results.

The fellow who loads his own shells has an advantage over the one who always buys factory-loaded shells, because he can develop loads for different game under various shooting conditions. He usually learns quickly that more powder or more shot does not always make a better pattern. In a 28 gauge over-and-under, for which I hand load, I get better patterns with ⅞ ounce shot than with either ¾ or one ounce. High velocity is not always a cure-all. It is the shot in the bird that counts. A good, even pattern is what you are looking for, one without holes, and you will find it easier to hit the target even if the shot is traveling a bit slower.

Loading your own shells provides another advantage for the scatter gunner, particularly the one who shoots a double with special loads. He can convert his modified and full choke into improved cylinder and modified and get tight patterns for more open bores.

If the pattern does not concentrate where you are looking, you may not be cheeking the comb of your gun as you should or the stock may need altering in length, pitch, comb height or thickness. Check with an experienced shooter or a gunsmith until the gun shows a pattern where you are looking.

Locating doves requires little practice; however, scout in the morning or late afternoon. They do not fly or feed in the middle of the day. If they are around, the hunter will see them in dead trees, on telephone or power line wires, taking gravel or in the feeding area. Doves usually concentrate around feed grounds, waterholes or roosts. They are gregarious birds and perch or fly

# Dove Shooting

in pairs or flights, numbers depending upon the concentration of doves in the vicinity.

Walking up feeding doves is very similar to hunting quail without a dog. Unlike a covey rise, however, doves get up in singles, doubles or staggered relays, as the hunter moves slowly along the feeding ground. Although its rising flight is not as fast as quail, the dove probably does more aerial acrobatics in the takeoff. One may rise rapidly and head for the trees, the next dove may be a straight-away, winging slowly just over the sunflower stalks, while the third may bank sharply, right or left.

Doves like almost any type of grain and will concentrate around fields, both before and after harvesting. The one seed that they like in this area is the seed from turkey mullein, or dove weed. They love it and shooting does not seem to drive them away. Milo maize, after it is harvested, always attracts doves, particularly after it is chopped up with a cultivator.

I remember a shoot while I was in Georgia, after bobwhite. Word got around that the doves were in a harvested field of peanuts. I was asked to participate and what a shoot we had! An interesting thing about that shoot, I remember, was that they have a small dove. They have the same dove that we have, but they also have a smaller one that certainly can fly and dart around. I hit a few, but my average was not to be bragged about.

Sunflower fields always attract doves and rarely fail to produce good shooting. One season, when hunting a sunflower field several times, I noticed that doves I cleaned had nothing but those seeds in their craws.

If you are hunting a strange territory, check the contents of the craw of a few doves to ascertain just what they are feeding on. This may give you better shooting on the next hunt. Regardless of cover or hunter approach, doves get up far enough away to provide a challenging range. Actually, I remember few doves shot up because of close range.

Shooting at doves coming to water or roost is difficult because of speed and range, and frequently roosting time comes after sundown, when hunting is illegal. Occasionally, however, the shooters can take a stand between the waterhole and roost, and get in some fast shooting before time runs out. The difficulty is, that as waterhole pressure increases, doves delay watering until it is too late to shoot. Fly away shooting, however, is the supreme challenge calling for "double the lead." Fly-away or path shooting appeals particularly to the experienced shooter who has learned, through the years, how to connect with the dove at maximum speed and at maximum range.

Ours is a livestock country in the hills and a farming country in the valley, so we have all kinds of dove shooting -- waterhole, feed and flight. At the waterhole, the flights are easy the first few days, and this is also true in the feeding area, but as time goes by the doves learn quickly and they come in later. The aerial antics eliminate any really easy shooting. Many shooters like to use a bit of cover, but not so much that vision is restricted. Cover should permit quick and easy standing with a full view in all directions. Personally, I seldom use a cover. One can remain absolutely still, until he is ready to shoot, and that fact will not cause the bird to change its course. Remember, keep still.

Doves frequently approach a waterhole down a draw and if there is a dead tree in the vicinity they will usually head for that perch. A hunter can take his stand near the dead tree and cover the area between the dead tree and the water.

A dead tree is an ideal place to locate decoys. One or more doves attract other doves, and decoys work very well indeed.

Even when several birds are approaching a waterhole, it is not often that all will follow the same flight pattern. Once the dove becomes suspicious, the aerial show begins, whether flying, swooping, dipping or ducking. The dove is a challenge

# Dove Shooting

for the hunter to place his shot load where the target will be when the shot string arrives.

Because of the speed and stamina of the dove, I do not like to stretch my gun or attempt shots which seem impossible. Many birds are wounded and lost because the hunter did not know that he had connected. Many doves carrying lead will fly beyond the hunter's range and then drop to the ground. Shooters should always watch the flight after the shot. You will be surprised how many more doves you will put in your game bag.

It is always necessary that the shooter carefully mark the bird down, or the point of fall, and retrieve as soon as possible because doves are hard to find in weeds or high grass.

During the early season, I usually find No. 8 field load to be all that is necessary. But, as the season progresses, I switch to No. 7½ with a heavier load.

It is difficult to overload a fast-flying dove, and I have very often scored by increasing the lead beyond that which seems adequate. Occasionally I have shot ahead of doves but, oh, how many times have I shot the tail feathers!

There are various types of swing in wing shooting and each type has its following, but it has always seemed to me that each man must learn for himself. Lead is something which no two may see in the same light. This I have learned. More shot loads find their way behind a flying dove than find their way too far ahead.

Dove speed of flight demands a lot of pre-season practice and clay targets provide the best solution. As the gap gradually narrows between expended shells and birds in the bag, the hunter will appreciate the hours spent with trap or skeet.

The dove is a fine game bird which also provides a rare flavored dish for the table, costly though it may sometimes be.

# 14 | Whitewings

My intense desire to have an outstanding shoot on the elusive whitewing is what led me to one of the finest weeks of shooting I have ever had. The whitewing is a member of the dove family. Considerably larger than our common mourning dove, weighing some 25 per cent to 50 per cent more, it has a few white feathers on each wing, from which it gets its name. It is a native of old Mexico, but some are found, and there is an open season, in the southern counties of California, namely Imperial and San Diego. It is found quite profusely in southern and western Arizona and in western Texas.

This bird flies fast but straight. It does not weave in flight like the common dove, but remember always to get ahead of the bird. Be sure you "double the lead." I had no trouble with my 28 gauge Parker, ⅞ ounces of No. 7½ shot, as long as the bird was within reasonable range. That seems to be the trouble with the inexperienced shooter. He does not allow the bird to get in range. He shoots at it too far away. This applies to most game -- doves, whitewings, and particularly ducks. As the old market hunter said, "Wait until you see the whites of their eyes, and then pull the trigger."

Now let me tell you how I received my invitation to participate in a whitewing shoot. I have been a member of the California Indians, a trapshooting organization, for many years. During that time, I had made the acquaintance of three of the finest sportsmen in Arizona -- namely, Glen Harrison, a propane dealer; Byron Kemp, a wholesale liquor dealer; and L.

M. White, a large contractor; all residents of Tucson, all high class trapshooters and real hunters. During the conversation in Reno, at the annual pow-wow of our organization, I expressed myself as wanting a whitewing shoot, because I had hunted most of the game of the United States, but had missed out on this particular game bird. I was invited and did not allow the invitation to remain vague or tentative. When the season opened, I wired them a reminder and received an immediate reply. We were fixed; the date was set.

I needed a shooting partner with whom to share my trip. Burrel Hyde and I had discussed the whitewing on many occasions and we had hunted together for some 30 years. So I called to advise him of the invitation. He, too, wanted to make the trip but could not leave until a certain hour, which necessitated taking a plane to Los Angeles to catch the American Airlines flight to Tucson.

We were met at Tucson by Glen Harrison and Byron Kemp, who delivered us to the Pioneer Hotel with instructions to be ready at 6:30 the next morning. L. M. White had been called out of the state but he left an enclosed Jeep for our use while in Tucson. It was exactly 6:30 when they drove up, and we were ready to go. Harrison, Kemp and another fine sportsman named Miles Abrams.

Since White was out of the city, Abrams had scouted north of town and had found a water hole at a dairy with many old trees up and down a dry wash, and he had obtained permission to hunt there. We sat around and waited until about eight o'clock, when the first of the birds came to the water. Then the heavens opened up and the whitewings poured in by the hundreds. Really, it was not much sport. The birds slowed up to get their drink, so I left the water hole and endeavored to get into a line of flight. But they came from every direction, and I did not have much luck. We finished out our limit in about an hour, after which we picked and cleaned our birds, washed our hands and headed for Tucson, taking the Jeep to see the sights and to await the next day for an evening shoot.

The next afternoon we headed south toward Nogales, Mexico. After traveling some 40 miles, we arrived at a large cattle range divided by a dry wash, lined with dead cottonwood trees, an ideal place for a dove shoot, but there was no game. We located a large concrete water tank full of water -- overflowing, in fact. We parked our car in the shade of a tree and waited for the evening flight. We did not have long to wait. At about five o'clock they began to come in droves from the west. The interesting thing to me was that the doves and whitewings were flying together, each in their natural flights. The doves were weaving from side to side, but the whitewings were flying straight. I could see little difference in speed between the two species.

We stationed ourselves some distance from the water hole, so that we could get the shooting at the maximum flight, and was it sport! The birds came from the west and over a considerable rise of ground so that they were against the sky when they came over us. It was perfect shooting, they were fine targets and we had few misses. That year the limit was 20 whitewings and we had no trouble filling our limit. Our trouble was that after the shoot they had to be dressed. We moved to a sandy, dry wash and found that a whitewing was not much more trouble than a dove. After covering our mess with sand, we washed our hands and returned to Tucson, still of the opinion that whitewings are an easier target than doves.

The next day we were to have another new experience. It was a dry year and there were few water holes, so Byron Kemp piloted his plane and found a fair size water hole, some miles south and west of Tucson, in the Indian reservation. We took our Jeep, filled with the five hunters and Mrs. Glen Harrison, wife of one of our hosts, and headed for the water hole. How

# Whitewings

*C. Burrel Hyde and the author -- two quail shooting partners who wanted to try whitewing shooting.*

they ever found it I will never know. There was no road, nothing but sagebrush and mesquite trees.

We arrived at our destination and it was ideal for a late afternoon shoot. There was a fair-sized pond of water, around which there was a strip of some 35 yards of bare ground surrounded by small mesquite trees. Mr. and Mrs. Harrison began making camp, so we knew something was up. We helped them set up a table and chairs and a barbecue in the shade of a nearby mesquite tree. They had a mess of the whitewings we had shot the previous day.

We each took a folding chair, set it up where we wanted to shoot and sat down and waited. We were admonished to look out for rattlesnakes, and it was a good thing that we were warned. All through the trees, evidently attracted by the water, were snakes; big ones, little ones, all sizes; I killed four while looking for a dead bird, so learned to drop the bird on open ground. If I could not I passed up the shot. We had no trouble getting our limit of 20 whitewings and I was glad indeed that I did not have my bird dog. I would have been scared to death for him; too many rattlers.

It was simply fantastic the way the birds poured into that pond of water, thousands upon thousands. Frankly, the shooting was just not much sport, sitting in a folding easy chair.

We finished shooting early, washed our hands with water the Harrisons brought with them and were ready for the wonderful dinner of whitewings Mrs. Harrison had prepared over the open fire. We finished about dusk and those Arizona drivers wound their way through the sagebrush without a guide and found Tucson. It was a wonderful end to a perfect whitewing shoot, hosted by big-hearted sportsmen of Arizona.

## 15 | Bandtail Pigeons

It was in 1895, and I was six years old, when my father took me out to the Hugh Hamilton blacksmith shop, about one-half mile north of Exter, California, and introduced me to bandtail pigeons. There were three large galvanized iron washtubs full of pigeons, each pigeon weighing over a pound.

The day before, word had reached town that the birds were in what was then the large grove of oak, some 3½ miles north of Exeter, feeding on acorns. Without much effort, a group of sportsmen was organized to go together and give the birds a reception the following afternoon. There was neither law nor limits on this bird at the time. The three tubs full of birds Dad showed me were the result of the afternoon shoot.

Anyone was welcome to a mess of pigeons, so we helped ourselves, together with the others, and headed for home. It was my job to pick and clean these birds, which I did without much effort, but they were bitter and not much value for food.

As I grew up, I remembered my first experience with bandtails and no effort to find a flight or shoot the bird just to be killing it. However, about 1932, some 37 years thereafter, the government purchased and paid the vineyardists for all grapes and left them on the vines, where they dried up as raisins. I was informed that the pigeons were coming into Mineral King Ranch, just east of Visalia, California, by the thousands.

The following Sunday it was raining, so with little to do I drove out to the Mineral King ranch in my "Sunday-go-to-meeting" clothes, stood in the rain until I was soaking wet and for a full two hours watched a sight I had never expected to see and probably will never see again: bandtail pigeons by the thousands.

There was a steady stream of birds about 100 yards wide as far as one could see and it seemed there was no end to the flight. It was unbelievable. Birds were everywhere, and when one realized that they weigh about one pound each, you can just imagine what they did to the small branches of a walnut tree, when some 300 or 400 pigeons settled down on the limb.

I noticed what was happening to the fruitwood, so went over to talk it over with Mr. McMillan, superintendent of the Visalia Orchard Company. He realized what was happening but was helpless because there was no open season and, of course, no limit allowed. We decided that I would get the game warden out to the ranch to see what was happening and what harm was being done and then, if permitted, get a few shooters who would be careful and not shoot up the trees. We might be able to scare them off.

Oliver Brownlow was the local game warden. I called that evening and made a date to see if he could go out with me and witness the flight the following afternoon. This we did, and with his permission, four of us went out Wednesday afternoon with plenty of ammunition. Our shooting group was composed of Jim Fluty, chief of police; Cy Parkin, the former baseball player; Charley Togni, stationer, and me. We had the fastest shoot in which it has ever been my privilege to participate. It was fast and furious. We finally ran out of ammunition, all of us, and we could see that we were not accomplishing our purpose. The pigeons kept coming by the thousands. We filled three barley sacks with the birds, which we took out to the county old people's home, and which, we were told later, they greatly enjoyed.

We learned that the bandtail pigeons were not an easy target. They can carry plenty of lead. I gave the first bird in the first

## Bandtail Pigeons

flock that came what I thought was the proper lead and killed the third bird back.

This reminded me of a dove shoot on the Grapevine Grade on the road to Badger and above Elderwood, north of Woodlake. The doves were coming down the canyon in high gear, going to feed. Tom Chatten, the old duck shooter, and his son Dick were on one side of the gully and Dave Douglas, the druggist, and I were on the other side. Dave was having his troubles when Tom Chatten yelled over, "Double the lead, Davey," which he did, and we finished our shoot with plenty of game for several dove pot pies.

We found that the flight of the bandtail pigeons is very deceptive. They fly much faster than they seem to be flying, besides taking a lot of lead, one certainly could and certainly should double the lead.

The shooting got away from the game warden. Oliver Brownlow simply could not police the situation and perhaps justly so, because the birds were really doing great damage to the walnut tress. Within but two or three days the area was alive with shooters, perhaps 100 or so. It sounded like a real battle. We tried it one evening and could not get a bird. They were picked up before our dog could retrieve them. We gave away the few we did get, but we did like to have the privilege. A few evenings later we were invited out for dinner, and we were served, of all things, wild pigeons! Boy, were they good! And why not? The birds were on relief and were being fed by Uncle Sam with the finest food obtainable.

After shooting near the roosting headquarters for three or four days with some 200 shooters daily, we decided to try the feeding grounds near Exeter. Young Milt Hadley heard of our plans and asked to be allowed to go with us, but his father, Josh Hadley, had grounded him for some six months before for leaving his gun fully loaded on the back porch. The gun was unloaded and put away with instructions not to touch it, and rightly so. It was a good lesson for the boy, but we convinced Josh that six months was long enough for a pretty good lesson, so he permitted the boy to go with us

He shot up all of his ammunition, so I loaned him my gun, gave him my shells and let him have the time of his young life.

Young Hadley was not the only one who used up his ammunition. Everyone did. I was told that shells were shipped to Visalia from Bakersfield and all other stations all the way to Stockton, California. One simply could not fathom the number of pigeons that were in the area. Where did they all come from, and where did they go? After about a month the birds left and all shooters, regardless of whether they were sportsmen, were left talking to themselves.

One thing that we learned about pigeons was that they would come into a decoy. We prepared wires and stooled birds on top of the grapestakes and, boy, did it work! When a bunch flew over, they came into shooting range, perhaps not the whole bunch, but one or more would break away and come into the stooled bird. It made great sport and there were few cripples. In later years, we put a pigeon decoy on a bamboo pole and placed it up through and at the top of live oak trees in the oak country where the birds were after the acorns. It always worked, but we shot fewer birds because they were bitter and it was much harder to make them palatable.

In later years we found that these birds roosted in the pine timber around 5,000 feet and in the early morning would usually fly over a gap or low place in the low mountains or hills going down into the oak timber country to feed. This occurred over a period of several years on Blue Ridge, east of Exeter, where some real shoots were obtained by various sportsmen.

I recall a shoot with Jim Fluty. We went into lower Grouse Valley, and climbed to the top of Blue Ridge early one morning, reaching there about daybreak. As it became light enough to see, we observed the birds coming from the east. Great flocks

## Bandtail Pigeons

of them came right at us low to the ground. We were forced to drop down the hill in order to get a shot that we could handle. A limit of 10 birds had been placed by the Fish and Game Commission and we had no trouble filling our limits.

We returned at a later date, Fluty wanting to try a .410 on the birds. We did, but without success. It was not enough gun or load. I have always used a 20 gauge with a fairly heavy load and one ounce of number 7 or 7½ shot and a 12 gauge would probably be better if the birds are flying any distance from the ground. It is a great bird to shoot and can be made palatable with some effort.

Very few upland shooters, except those living in the flyways of those elusive and sporty birds, have any knowledge of bandtail pigeon shooting. The beginner is due for an awakening and shooting experience he will not soon forget, when he shoots his last of perhaps two boxes of shells he brought along. He probably will ask an experienced shooter, "How far do you lead them?" The answer, is, "Twice as far as you think, then double it."

Pigeon shooting is different from most other types of upland bird shooting in that it is mostly pass shooting.

Bandtails fly to feed on acorns, berries, fruit, dry seeds, nuts and so forth. They fly in flocks of from a few birds to perhaps three or four dozen. They roost mainly in high trees and in high areas which they leave early in the morning, at dawn, flying in flocks of 10 to 15 to 50 or more. They are usually through feeding about 9 a.m., after which they loaf or roost in local areas where there is stubble field or cut wheat near hilly areas. You may find them feeding there, in which case you will need to set up your blinds near these fields the day before you shoot. You will never get near enough to jump shoot as you would do with doves.

Bandtail pigeons are unpredictable. They do not always use the same flyways and may be in great numbers one year and very scarce the next. It seems that they are governed by the food supply. They are fond of pinon nuts, madrone berries, acorns, and so forth.

Early in the morning, they fly along the contour of the land, usually seeking a saddleback or low spot between the hills. Their incoming flight approaching these passes is slower and the shooting angle much better. Experienced hunters, therefore, like to station themselves on the ridges of such flyways, well hidden, and shoot as the birds approach. Those shooters unable to reach the summit will find that their shots are longer and the birds speed much faster after they have crossed over the ridge and begin to drop down to the feeding areas.

If this is your first shoot and you want to hunt bandtail pigeons successfully, may I suggest that you hunt with an experienced hunter. Although the limit is eight birds, take plenty of shells, perhaps four boxes. You may need them all. If you don't, someone else will.

Some information on the birds' habits, both migratory and feeding, may be helpful. They usually roost at the high elevations, in large flocks, preferring high, relatively leafless trees as protection from hawks. Early in the morning they break up into small groups, swooping down to the lower elevations, to feed on acorns, nuts, berries and fruits. They prefer tree feeding; however, they may feed in grain fields if the fields are nearby and tree feeding is scarce.

While you may see a few birds flying in midmorning, if you haven't a limit by ten o'clock you probably should wait until the late afternoon, after four o'clock.

The important rule in hunting pigeons is to first find the bandtails. This sport is well worth a scouting trip a day or two before the opening day. Get there at dawn and observe the flights; look for a saddleback or ridge. I suggest that you build a blind out of weeds or limbs. Put your name on it in case another

## Bandtail Pigeons

finds it before you get there the next morning. Wear a camouflage jacket and cap and, above all, hold still as the birds approach, or they will veer away, making a longer and more difficult shot, as well as making it harder to retrieve your bird.

If you have a good dog, take him along. He will find your birds and, in all probability, others as well.

I much prefer a full choke 20 gauge double or one with a modified right and a full choke left. If you shoot an automatic or pump be sure it is plugged. Three shots are all that you are entitled to have. Otherwise, you and a game warden may have an unpleasant discussion.

As to ammunition, you cannot be over-gunned with these birds. Shot magnums 1½ oz. in a 12 gauge are your best bet, regular 1½ oz. express loads should do the job or even number 7½ trap loads for the close shots.

Take plenty of shells. If you limit out eight birds with 50 shells you are either a better than average shot or your shooting opportunities were good. If your gun chambers a three-inch shell, take three-inch magnums with No. 6 shot, and don't be ashamed to use them.

The surest way to ruin a shoot for yourself and nearby shooters is to shoot at birds out of range, and this applies also to shooting ducks. A shotgun is a 40-yard weapon. Few shooters can hit a fast-flying bird at 50 yards, almost none at 60 yards.

Forty yards is 120 feet, not a great distance. Thirty yards is your best distance, so hold your fire. Hold still and let them come in. If they are flying your way, you will get your share and you will not ruin the other shooters' chances. Don't sky bust.

The reason bandtail pigeons rarely feed after midmorning is that, unlike chukar partridges or other birds, they have no crops. They fill their enlarged throats or gullets, then must rest while digesting their food. I have downed many a pigeon so full of acorns that one is protruding from its mouth.

# 16 | An Oregon Shoot

In the early 1930's, Malheur County, Oregon, had gained quite a reputation for pheasant hunting. So Lynn Colomb, the bird shooter from New Orleans who had been raised with a 12 gauge Fox and a long-sleeved hunting coat, and I decided to go. Colomb made arrangements with Charles Parker, of Parker-Schram Company of Portland, Oregon, contractors who built the concrete pontoon bridge across Lake Washington at Tacoma, to meet us in Ontario, the county seat of Malheur County. We met there at the Moore Hotel a couple of days before the opening. Parker had made arrangements with several farmers for shooting privileges on their ranches. We spent the next day or two visiting farmers and exercising dogs.

We opened on a ranch about five miles west of Ontario on the road to Vale, Oregon, and on the south side of the Malheur River. What an opening day! We were out early. The pheasants were squawking when the opening time arrived. We were in a 60-acre alfalfa field and hunting in an easterly direction. When we had walked one-half mile through the field, we were through. Each of us had a limit of four pheasants, all cocks, even though we were allowed one hen in each limit.

The Idaho season opened three days after the Oregon season and we hunted Idaho after trying the dogs in the beet fields, where we seemed to get more dog work than in the regular haunts. After obtaining our Idaho license we had no trouble getting permission from the farmers, and we were all set. We could see little difference in the hunting whether we hunted the

## An Oregon Shoot

east or the west side of the Snake River. The birds seemed to be everywhere. It was fun to drive into the country late in the evening and watch the pheasants fly across the river or onto the islands in the middle of the stream.

Pheasant shooting in this area was too easy in those days, so each of us was fairly glad to get it over with when Charlie Parker headed for Portland and we headed for Klamath Falls. Our birds had been shipped, so we were free to do as we pleased. Colomb had a contact in the Main Hotel. The clerk was a quail hunter, so we found him after checking in, but he advised that the quail crop was low that year, that he had bagged only four birds in a full day's hunt.

I took the lead and said, "Colomb, I have an acquaintance here. Let me see what I can do." I took the phone and called my friend Paul Landry, a former president of the Oregon Insurance Association at the same time I was president of the California Association. Landry took no more than 10 minutes getting to the hotel. When he walked into our room, Colomb almost fainted. He had known my friend in Donaldsonville, Louisiana.

Landry was not a hunter but had a large acquaintance in the area. He promised to get on the phone that evening and give our problem a try. After a nice visit he went home and we went to dinner and then to our room. About nine o'clock the phone rang and it was Landry. He said, "You are all set." He gave me instructions and directions. We hit the hay. It all led to one of the finest quail hunts and visits it has ever been my privilege to enjoy. I must tell you about it.

We drove into the yard at the appointed hour, and a man was feeding his dogs in a kennel about 100 yards from the house. We spoke and he grunted, advising us to go on to the house. We did and met his wife, a very gracious, hospitable lady. He came in some 10 or 15 minutes later and introduced himself as Charles Leister, one of the partnership known as Leister Brothers, of which I will tell you more later in this chapter.

After some time visiting, Leister said, "If you don't mind, I would like to go along with you." I said, "Of course, we expected you to be with us if you enjoy hunting. We have two pointers which we hope will do their stuff."

We were off. We drove not over a quarter of a mile when he stopped with, "They should be near here." We climbed the fence, turned our dogs loose and, so help me, they froze, but the birds were running and flushed wild and out of range. We fired our guns into the air and watched the birds fan out on a hillside not too far away. We followed. Colomb's dog froze up. He offered the first shot to Leister, who refused, so Lynn kicked the birds out and made a beautiful double. We looked to the right and there was California Jubilee on point. Leister again refused the shot, so I walked in, stroked my dog, and again two birds went into the air. My little 28 gauge Parker spoke twice and again the birds hit the grass. They were California quail in Oregon and in a covey of probably 200 birds.

Leister had started back to the car when I called to find out if something was wrong. He said, "No, but I am going to put my gun up and watch you fellows shoot," and he did just that.

We had a day when it seemed impossible to miss, but with birds flushing under point and in the open, why should a bird be missed?

We soon had our limits, 15 birds each, when Leister said, "Would you like to see my ranch?" We said that we would be honored, and you can't blame him for wanting to show it off. It was a beauty. He told us that we were the first to shoot his quail. He had started with 12 birds that he had purchased from a pet shop some four years previously, and they had multiplied to the present number in this short time.

At that time we estimated that there were probably 500 birds in the five coveys we flushed, some of which may have been native birds, because they were known to have been in existence at the time of the original plant, but in very small

## An Oregon Shoot

quantities. We were shown his trout ponds, a beautiful setup consisting of small streams and pools literally alive with rainbow trout.

The streams and ponds had been stocked with a small shrimp that he had imported from the east and they had multiplied most profusely. After this exhibition of what could be accomplished with trout, we were shown his private duck club. It was a sight to behold, alive with mallard, sprig, widgeon, spoonbills, and teal. They were there by the hundreds, a sight to make any sportsman's heart flutter and our trigger fingers become numb. It was out of season, so we had to be content to just look.

We were driven around the range to see the pumping plants with 12-inch discharges throwing great streams of water to supplement the ditches flowing from the Lost River, which runs through the valley. It was a sight to behold for me, coming from the San Joaquin Valley.

It was nearing noon, so I suggested that we better be going. We did not want to impose on our host. He said that we would drive up to the house, which we did, and were ushered into the house, where Mrs. Leister insisted that we stay for lunch. Boy, what a lunch for a couple of hungry hunters! We simply could not break away and did not leave the ranch until after four o'clock, with the most pleasant memories of a real quail shoot.

# 17 | Grouse and Hungarian Partridge

My intense desire to hunt the pinnated grouse, commonly called the prairie chicken, in 1946 led me to study the game laws of the various states where the birds were found, but to no avail. The bird was almost extinct in the United States, but I found that there was an open season in Saskatchewan, Canada, so I talked three of my shooting partners into joining me in a trip to the prairies in that part of the world.

I knew that Ray Holland, editor of *Field and Stream Magazine*, had hunted the area for several years, so he was contacted and he praised the area highly, particularly as it pertained to the Hungarian partridge and the sharp-tailed grouse.

It is not very often that four men, two of whom were still active in business, can leave together and not be obligated to rush things and be back at a certain time, but we had such a foursome. It was composed of Lucien V. Schmittou, a retired orange grower from Porterville, California, a fine sportsman; "Cy" Parkin, who at that time resided in Iowa; R. J. "Dick" Chatten, a shooting partner from Hanford, and myself, all avid game hunters who had hunted together on many occasions.

One cannot hunt successfully without a dog, so we decided that Chatten's pointer and my pointer Rex would be the dogs to take.

A fair-sized, two-wheel trailer was purchased and a twin doghouse installed, with plenty of room left for odds and ends, together with our ammunition, dog food and sundries. It trailed

## Grouse and Hungarian Partridge

perfectly, so we headed out early in September, 1946, through Nevada to Elko, north into Idaho, picking up Cy Parkin at Twin Falls, then north through Sun Valley and Salmon, Idaho, over the Continental Divide, into the Bitterroot Valley in Montana.

We camped on the west fork of the Bitterroot River to rest a few days and do some hunting and fishing, the object of our trip. I had fished this stream, always with great success, but this time it was a real effort. Lucien Schmittou was high man, probably because he was the most expert with a fly, at least the wet fly. I was a dry-fly fisherman and the others were just fishermen. However, we had all the trout we could use, so we were well satisfied.

The second day we spent hunting a grouse in that part of the country, with fair success, but not much sport. It was about the size of a bantam chicken, reddish-brown in color, and that year there were a great many in that part of Montana. They seemed to like the pine trees, about 100 feet high, and did not seem to like to fly. We would not pot them, so one man would shoot near the bird to flush it and the other man got to shoot him. We took turns to be fair.

The next morning we awoke in a snowstorm so broke camp and went into Hamilton, Montana, for breakfast and then to Missouri, where we headed east to Miles City and wound up at Bozeman, where Cy Parkin had a friend, with whom he had been a partner in his younger days, who was now a large cattleman near town. He came down to see us and invited the four of us to watch him load 12 carloads of shorthorn cattle. We went, and it was a sight! All were the same size and, to me, looked exactly alike. I could not believe that one man could own so many, each looking like the other.

After a fine visit we headed for Plentywood, Montana, a small town in the northeast corner of that great state, near the

Canadian border. Why it was named Plentywood I will never know; there was not a tree within 50 miles of the town.

That evening we went out to take in the town and, of course, found a crap game. I was following Cy Parkin with $10 a throw and he shot nine straight craps which, of course, cost me $90. We tried to double our bets but were not permitted to do so. We walked out and went to our hotel for a good night's rest before entering Canada.

The next morning we entered Saskatchewan without difficulty because we had previously obtained all the necessary papers, such as the proof that the dogs had been vaccinated recently and the automobile license, and paid the duty on our ammunition which, incidentally, amounted to something over $40, because we had shells for guns from my 28 gauge to a 12 gauge, including the 20 gauge and a 16 gauge. We were prepared because the shooting was going to be new to us.

We proceeded to Regina, the capital of the province of Saskatchewan, where we obtained our licenses and received the most pleasant treatment from the game wardens and other individuals in the Department of Fish and Game. They warned us not to shoot their wild turkey which, upon questioning, turned out to be the sandhill crane which had become quite scarce but was making a comeback.

We went by the home of Mr. H. Felts, who had been recommended to us by the Fish and Game people and the Field and Stream Publishing Company, which had made our reservations in Imperial, a small town some 75 miles north of Regina. En route we also visited the city of Moosejaw and found it to be a very clean place with wide streets and, at that time, very busy and prosperous.

We reached the little town of Imperial in the early afternoon and, with little trouble, found the Imperial Hotel, a small, two-story frame building with 18 rooms which was very clean and orderly. This hotel was owned and operated by two young

## Grouse and Hungarian Partridge

Canadians who could not do enough to make us happy and comfortable.

After a short walk around the town to get oriented, I returned to the hotel and was sitting in the lobby when a small Scotsman came over and sat down, opening up a conversation with, "American hunters?" I said "Yes" and could see that he was lonely, as his wife was in a hospital in Regina. His two young daughters were working and away from home all day. He said, "I am not working now and will be glad to show you where the game can be found."

We agreed to meet the next morning at eight o'clock and look for some sharp-tail and pinnated (*Tympanuchus Cupido*) grouse, which he said would be out in the bluffs.

I must tell you something that happened on our first day in Imperial. It was the opening of the goose season and I ran into a friendly young Canadian goose hunter who had looked for additional 16 gauge shells. He had shot three boxes, or 75 times, and did not have his limit, so he was in town looking for an additional supply, but without avail. I knew that Cy Parkin had a 16 gauge and plenty of 16 gauge shells, so I went to the hotel, found Cy (knowing that he had expressed himself as wanting to shoot a honker) and they made a trade, a box of shells for the use of his blind the next morning. They were both very happy.

Cy was up early the next morning, going alone to the blind on the shore of a small lake. He had the time of his life, bringing back five Canadian honkers before noon, each weighing from 10 to 14 pounds. Of course, we could not use the game, but rationing was in effect throughout Canada so we had no trouble giving the meat away. However, we kept two and found it about the best meat served to us on our stay in Imperial. To say that we enjoyed it, together with others in the hotel, would be putting it mildly.

Cy's morning for geese delayed us one day for our trip to the bluffs, but the second day we loaded up the four hunters, the Scotsman and the two dogs and, under the direction of our guide, headed west. We were out about five miles when our host yelled, "There they are." Of all things, there were five good-sized birds in a stubblefield a few feet off the side of the road. Dick Chatten was on the front seat with me. I was driving. We grabbed our guns, stopped the car and headed for the stubblefield. Two birds flushed wild but three were in the air and within range. Dick took on the right bird and I made a double on the two straight-aways. We retrieved and almost fainted. The birds were the true prairie chicken or pinnated grouse. We were flabbergasted, to say the least, Dick looked at me and I looked at him. It was our first and I am sure our last because we were ashamed of ourselves.

We had gone a good many miles to get one and then wished we had not. There was so much other game and the true prairie chicken was so scarce that we were indeed sorry that we had connected. I understand that there now are a few states in the United States where they have made a small comeback and where they have a short open season. At present, the longest seasons are in Nebraska, South Dakota, Oklahoma, Kansas and Texas. Think of it! The same bird that flushed in waves ahead of sportsmen and market hunters until the world of grouse was destroyed by the plow. It then adapted itself to the grain fields, but the pressure of civilization almost destroyed it.

We had so many plans to do what we had just done, and now we were sorry that we had accomplished our objective. We had a meeting right in the middle of the road, talked it over and agreed that we would spend our time on sharp-tail grouse and Hungarian partridges.

We were only a few miles out when our Scottish guide stopped us in the middle of a great willow patch. I asked him where the bluffs were. He answered, "You are in them." They

## Grouse and Hungarian Partridge

call a willow patch a bluff in that part of the world. Perhaps, before we go further, I should explain something that we learned about the game we were after. The Hungarian partridge and the sharp-tailed grouse are often called the prairie chicken in that area.

The sharp-tail grouse, the relative of the true prairie chicken, is holding its own and is increasing in some areas. We found them quite plentiful in the area we were hunting, particularly in the so-called bluffs, with coveys of perhaps 100 birds. They are an easy shot. I made several right and lefts with my little 28 gauge Parker.

There is a quickly noted difference in the two birds, the true prairie chicken and the sharp-tail. The true prairie chicken has a barred breast while the sharp-tail is flecked. The sharp-tail will roost in trees and will take advantage of heavy cover, although a dozen or so olive brown eggs are laid in a ground nest. Flying, the sharp-tail shows considerable white. This species prospers sufficiently on farms and ranches so that several states have opened seasons.

Besides in the bluffs we found sharp-tail around abandoned farm houses and skeletons of old abandoned farm machinery with weeds growing around that formed a perfect protection from hunters and weather.

In late September and early October the sharp-tail follow a warm weather pattern. In the morning they feed either in the stubblefields or around the wild rose bush. They like the snowberry, silver berry, buck brush and rose bush.

The other game bird we hoped to learn something about was the "Hun." Its true name is the European gray partridge. It is plentiful in the grain fields of Hungary, and some of the more successful plantings in America have originated here in Alberta. Some of these successful plantings are in Oregon, Washington, Idaho and Alberta, from which they have spread to neighboring provinces in Canada and to other states in the United States.

I have never had too much success in sport with the Hun. It flushes wild to a good quail dog. I have often thought that a wild, fast pointer could pin one down, but I have never seen it happen. All that I grassed were long shots or birds that happened to fly by us when flushed. I notice that the Hun will fly over the brow of the rising ground and go to the ground immediately thereafter. If the hunter will follow the bird's flight, he will make the additional flush when over the brow of the hill. After the second or third flush, sometimes he will stick and one may get a point and a shot within range.

I have hunted this bird in Malheur County and Harney County, Oregon and found that they are somewhat similar to the habits of the chukar partridge there. They do not fly uphill. Along the Malheur River we found that we could hunt them on the slopes on each side of the stream, one shooter at the top, one half-way down and one at the bottom. A Hun would flush and always fly straight down so we took turns and changed positions occasionally. It was quite successful and good sport, but no dog work. Another day, at a distance, I noticed two hunters hunting with dogs and they were getting some shooting. They were so far away, I could not tell what they were using, so I decided to investigate and find out. After walking over very close to where they were, I could see that they had toy balloons tied to each of their shoulder straps in back of their heads.

I walked over and introduced myself and asked them just what this was all about. They were friendly and courteous and explained that the Huns evidently thought the balloons were hawks and went to cover. The hunters were getting some great sport with their dogs. Two years later we obtained some gas and some toy balloons and headed for Malheur County to try our luck with artificial hawks, but with no luck. The wind blew so

## Grouse and Hungarian Partridge

hard the full time we were there we could not get the balloons overhead. We spent our time with pheasants.

Getting back to the Canadian provinces, we had little luck with the Huns from a sportsman's point of view; there was no dog work. There were plenty of birds, and we obtained our share. The birds flushed wild so they were all long shots; about all our dogs could do was retrieve. Frankly, I remember but one point.

I must tell you about an experience with the Hun, something that was new to us Californians. Chatten, Schmittou and Buckman drove up to Watrus, a little town some 30 miles north of our headquarters in Imperial. It had snowed the night before, and the snow was about eight inches deep everywhere.

We had reached within about three miles of Watrus when a covey of Huns flew over the road in front of us and landed in the snow to our left. We parked and reached for our guns and headed for where we thought the birds landed, some dozen of them. We reached the spot but there were no birds -- at least, that was what we thought. Then one exploded right at our feet. Chatten was ready and nailed it right in front of Schmittou. Then I noticed a blow-hole where I kicked the snow and out came another. It was no target. I dropped it within 40 feet of where I stood. Between us we snowed nine Huns out of a possible dozen birds and were satisfied. We passed up the others and went on to Watrus, but it was an experience none of us ever expected to have.

Upon our arrival in Watrus we found the meeting place of the Rotary Club, but their program did not reach there on account of the snow. They asked us to fill in and tell about California, which we did, and they seemed very pleased. We drove to Imperial that night in a snowstorm and headed south for North and South Dakota the next morning. It was a wise decision we made, because we could have been snowed in there for some days. We fought the snow until we reached the southern boundary of North Dakota. The snow driving was over as soon as we hit South Dakota, and were we glad.

As we rolled out of Saskatchewan into North Dakota we were still in about a foot of snow. We drove clear through the state, with snow in various depths. When we hit the line between North and South Dakota we were again on dry ground. It was a grand and glorious feeling for a group of California hunters.

We pulled into Herrold, South Dakota, to meet Elmore Parkin, Cy Parkin's nephew, and Jack Bohling, with whom Cy had made our reservations. Two finer young hunters one has never met, and they were as interested as each member of our party. Reservations had been made in Miller, South Dakota, a larger town some miles from Harold.

Let me tell you something about conditions in South Dakota at the time. The state was at its peak in pheasant production. Every newspaper and magazine was full of articles on the pheasant population. Businessmen, restaurants, hotel owners, sporting goods stores, rooming houses and it seemed everyone, except the farmers, were extending invitations to come and shoot pheasants.

Just to show the crowded conditions in every area where the pheasants were in such profusion, I will tell you we were in a three-story, old home with 42 other hunters and two bathrooms. It was a good thing that we could not shoot in that state that year until high twelve. There were not enough eating places so the hungry hunters were backed up for a block or more waiting for their turn.

We were two days ahead of the opening so had arranged to meet Parkin and Bohling the next noon to arrange with them for our opening shoot and to get a license. We were there as scheduled and they suggested a ride into the country, which was agreeable to all concerned.

We went west and south to the area known as the Big Bend of the Missouri River. It was about five o'clock in the afternoon

## Grouse and Hungarian Partridge

*Claude Bohning and C. V. Parkin, our hosts and guides -- goose hunters, but they knew their pheasants.*

and there were pheasants running and flying everywhere. They must have been disturbed by something. Looking toward the setting sun, I would have wagered that there were 1,500 birds in the air at one time. It was a sight -- one that I never expect to see again.

That year shooting started at noon. The next day we met our new friends and drove north into a cornfield not over a mile from town. There we unloaded dogs, hunters, guns and desire. We loaded our guns and soon there were the two dogs on point but no birds. They were on a running scent. That farmer had strip-farmed with the corn some 75 yards wide and then summer fallowed. It was great for hunters because pheasants do not like to run in the open. They stay in the cover. The fields are approximately half a mile long with open ground at each end. Our friends put two shooters at the end, and the rest of us made the drive from one end to the other. We could see birds ahead of us and the dogs on point most of the time. The pheasants ran our quail dogs crazy.

Not much happened until we reached within 100 yards of the end, when it seemed the whole landscape raised and the air was full of pheasants. Two doubles and a single and a shooter had his limit, which was five per day. Chatten and I were through, but we made an additional drive and all were ready to see the sights.

For a meat-hungry hunter it was fabulous. For a bird dog man it just was not for pointers and setters. We had our fun with the dogs in the evening, out on the prairie, in the buffalo grass. There were plenty of birds, mostly hens which we did not shoot, but one could get his limit of roosters in an hour. It was more like quail shooting.

Using the technique learned from my old shooting friend, Dan Calcote, of counting three when the pheasant flushes from a dog on point, we had no trouble killing pheasants. The tendency is to shoot too fast, which causes one to undershoot.

Frankly, I do not remember seeing as many poor sportsmen in my life as I saw in South Dakota. They had come from all corners of North America. I saw a car drive up to a farmer's fence, the driver jump out with a set of wire snippers and cut the wires. The car was driven into the field and out the same

## Grouse and Hungarian Partridge

way on the other side. Several head of stock got out on the highway, so we drove back and then went into the house to advise the owner. He was very appreciative and even offered to go with us and get our limits!

I met another farmer whose hobby was shooting geese. He had saved some wingtipped Canadian honkers, nursed them back to good health and had them in his barnyard. They say that they will never mate again, but he swore that they did and that they raised five young geese, which were just about ready to fly when one of the visiting so-called sportsmen stopped his car, shot the young geese, threw them over the fence and into his car and sped away. The farmer had tears in his eyes while telling us about the episode.

One afternoon we came in early, delivered our birds to the poultry plant for cleaning and decided to go inside and look around. The plant was approximately 40 by 100 feet and was covered with pheasants to approximately four feet high, in bundles of five with the name of the hunter on each bundle. This will give you some idea of the birds killed each day or two and the business for the plant as well as the work for the residents of Miller, South Dakota. We understood that there were four such plants in that little town. It was great for the townspeople but not so good for the farmer. However, I do want to say that I have never met a finer or more friendly man than the South Dakota farmer. We never trespassed. We had a farmer's permission before we went onto his land to hunt, and we were never turned down. After five days of this and being somewhat anxious to get back to California and home, Parkin left for Iowa, we thanked our hosts and started for California.

# 18 | Wild Turkey

All my adult shooting life, I have wanted a crack at the wild turkey. I have read of the bird from the earliest days of the pilgrims and the New Englanders; how the bird was abundant in almost all of the eastern and southern states; how they were hunted in various localities by calling them or by waiting at their roosting tree and getting what was needed as they came to roost. I read of all these various hunting methods and experiences, how our ancestors went to the woods each year for what they thought was necessary to celebrate Thanksgiving Day.

I also read of how the wild turkeys became depleted; how the open seasons were closed in almost all of the states and then how the game departments of the various states began to raise and release them with very good results. I understand that Pennsylvania's program was one of the first and most successful. Other states had success and open seasons were allowed, one by one, in various states across the country until we now have an open season on wild turkeys in California.

I read that one of the first states to open in the west was Arizona, but the restriction that stopped me was that one could not use a shotgun, only a rifle. This did not interest me, so I refrained from hunting turkeys in Arizona.

The next try was in New Mexico. I went there with the hope that I would get a shot at the king or queen of all game birds in America. Again I was stopped. They would not let an outsider hunt their wild turkeys, and I do not believe they were wrong. They were the ones to bring the hunting of this bird back to New Mexico sportsmen, not me. I next sought a turkey in Georgia but they, too, had a rule similar to the one in New Mexico: outsiders could not hunt the turkey.

Some time later I heard that they were raising and releasing the wild turkey to shoot on the Madera-Fresno Shooting Club. I had hunted pheasants, chukars, guinea hens and bobwhite quail at the club on various occasions. It is located between Fresno and Madera some miles west of Highway 99, and it is well managed. I called them and made arrangements for a wild turkey shoot.

Some days later, Jim Ingle of Tulare, my shooting partner for the day, and I took Sport, the finest bird dog that I have ever owned, loaded ourselves into my four-wheel drive Scout and departed for the Madera-Fresno shooting preserve with the hope of killing my first wild turkey.

We checked in at headquarters fairly early and were informed as to the area that would be the most probable area for our attempt. Jim was working the dogs and I was driving the Scout because I am unable to walk any considerable distance. We worked east to west and back again picking up some points and shots on both chukars and pheasants. Sport was working perfectly.

Both Jim and I were in perfect timing that day, neither failing to make a shot. When Jim yelled "Point" and I drove over, there was Sport, stiff as a poker, on a beautiful point and trembling from head to foot. He was some 10 feet from a small bunch of tumbleweeds to my right. Jim said, "Get out, it is your shot," when it seemed that the whole pile of weeds exploded and there was that big turkey flying east and right in front of me. Boy, did I take careful aim! I did not want to mutilate the bird and shoot it in the side at that distance so I carefully covered its head with my 20 gauge Parker Brothers and pulled the trigger. The big bird fell dead with its head

*Fresno Madera Preserve, 1966.*

almost shot away. It hardly quivered. Sport went to retrieve, but it was all new to him. He was like my dog with blue grouse on Redwood Mountain years before. He took it by the neck and dragged it to me. I do not know who was the most happy, Sport or myself.

Some days later, Jim Ingle and I invited Harrell J. Harrell to the same club in Madera County. We again went after a turkey as well as other game. We started hunting in a westerly direction and had bagged both pheasants and chukars when we reached the west end of the field and had moved south surrounding a small reservoir. Ingle was on the south side and I was on the west side and Harrell was on the east when it seemed that the reservoir had exploded and there was our turkey, flying east from me toward Harrell. I did not want to shoot the bird up

## Wild Turkey

too badly so took careful aim, trying to shoot off the left wing. I pulled the trigger but the bird kept going. I had missed when I heard a second shot and Harrell had shot the bird stone dead. It fell at his feet.

The bird had flushed wild from the heavy undergrowth in the dry reservoir. It, too, was a beautiful bird. We did not get a point. Sport was working further south.

The surprising thing to me was the speed that these big birds could get off the ground and their flight after getting into the air. To me it is phenomenal. Perhaps the ones that we shot had not been killed in Alabama, Georgia or New Mexico, but I tell you that they were one of the shooting thrills of my life. There is one reservation, however. I think I still prefer the big, broad-breasted turkey for the table to these wild birds of some 13 pounds.

# 19 | Sage Hen or the Sage Grouse

The game bird most numerous and widespread on the desert and sage brush plains of the west is what is called the sage hen. It is also probably the least known upland game bird. The sage hen is the largest of all American grouse. The only bird larger than the sage hen is the wild turkey.

Fully grown male birds may weigh as much as eight pounds. In the field, the birds give a very dark, heavy appearance. Their actual color is mottled gray-brown. Their most distinctive feature is a tail composed of many long pointed feathers.

When flushed these birds get up slowly. They are capable of long flights at speeds of 45 to 50 miles per hour. Since their diet consists chiefly of the tender shoots, leaves and seeds of the sage brush, they are almost never found at any other type of cover.

The daily movements of the sage hens are fairly regular, very similar to the California quail. You will find them in about the same location each day. In the morning they leave the ridges and move down to the dry gullies to the nearest water, after which they move back into the sage brush, spreading out to feed and slowly drifting up towards higher ground. Near midday they settle down, sometimes in larger numbers, to rest in the shade of heavy cover, to be on the move again in the late afternoon.

Early in the morning and late in the afternoon, the birds may be located by following the dry catch basins and streams, but only those that are bordered by heavier sage cover. While these hours offer the best chance for finding the birds, it is sometimes

## Sage Hen or the Sage Grouse

difficult to get a good shot. The birds flush readily and rather often out of range if they have been hunted. However, on opening day or on territory that has not been hunted, it is often possible to approach the moving birds openly to get a good shot.

At mid-day the hunting becomes more difficult, but the shooting improves over the vast stretches of rolling sage brush hills. One might conclude that finding birds in such an area would be impossible. It does require effort and often a good deal of walking, but it is not impossible.

Sage hens in certain areas of Northern California, Northeastern California, Nevada, Eastern Oregon, Eastern Washington, Idaho and parts of Montana are numerous, and the sign is readily identified.

Under certain conditions, including some hunting pressure, the birds will not be found far from water. Therefore, by walking the dry draws that lead to the water, the high ground on both sides of the stream and in circles around the catch basin, it should be possible to locate the heavier signs that indicate a roosting or dusting area. Some signs should be in evidence in good sage hen country. When the sign is found, hunters should spread out and walk to the draws that lead into the area. Mid-day hunting, if successful, provides good shooting. The birds tend to sit tight even under heavy hunting pressure, flushing only to a good bird dog or at the approach of the hunter's foot.

Some hunters claim that a sage hen will ruin a good bird dog. The birds are hard for a dog to retrieve and tend to make a dog hard-mouthed. If a dog is properly trained, it will retrieve anything. They also claim that any unwounded birds smell so strongly of sage that the dog's nose is almost useless. While there may be some truth in these claims, I have used three different dogs on sage hen and I have yet to see one ruined or fail to bring in a bird. It is true that the dog may have difficulty picking up a sage hen because of the bird's thick, sticky feathers, but my pointers have never refused. One of them got hold of a bird's head and dragged it to me like my pointer Sport did with my first wild turkey. Obviously, he could not get it into his mouth so he did the next best thing, but he got it to me.

Frankly, many sage hen hunters do not use dogs. I doubt if I would ever go hunting without one. Walking and watching a good dog is the greatest thrill of upland shooting.

The hunter trained on pheasant or other upland game may easily miss his first shot at this game. These birds get up slowly, and even on cross shots a lead is seldom necessary if the shots are taken while the bird is fairly close. Their speed builds up rapidly, and once they are well underway good leads will be needed. It is this variation in speed that makes the sage hen a sporting target.

While the sage hen is a large bird, it is soft feathered, and therefore not a particularly hard bird to kill. I prefer a 20 gauge, as I do on ducks, with a heavy load of 6 or 7½ shot.

Many hunters refuse shots on the larger birds, claiming that a full grown sage hen is too tough and too strong to eat. It is true that the younger birds are delicious eating and some of the older ones can be very tough indeed. However, I would not pass up a shot just because the bird was large. I have found that the breast meat of even the oldest bird can be tenderized and fried in thin strips for very delicious eating.

The sage hen season often coincides with other upland game such as pheasant, Hungarian partridge, chukars, or sharptail grouse. Sage hen hunting, when combined with other upland game, can be a great deal of pleasure on a hunting trip.

My first introduction to the sage hen was with R. J. (Dick) Chatten, my old shooting partner from Hanford. We went primarily for the experience of shooting sage hen, but took my fly rods along and did some fly fishing in the West Walker River near Bridgeport, California.

Our hunting was done with dogs on the long slope south of the river. My memory is that it was in the latter part of August and the birds were about four-fifths grown. It was our first experience with the birds, but we ran into another hunter, George Hinds, whom I had met before near Exeter and who was related to the Horace Davis family. Hinds had no dogs, so we invited him to hunt with us. He accepted, and we shot together for three or four days. Hinds was an old sage hunter and was willing to teach Dick and me the fine points of hunting sage hens, previously told in this chapter. We had no trouble either in finding birds or bringing them down after we did find them. Neither did our dogs have much trouble with the birds. We had many a point and found the birds to be a fairly easy target.

We were staying in Bridgeport and had no trouble giving our birds away. The people of that small community seemed glad to get them.

For some years the sage hen was a fairly scarce bird. The season was closed in California for some time, but has since been opened for a short period in certain locations. We hunted them near Andrews, north of Winnemucca, Nevada, with fair success, and later on the west road through Fields and west of Andrews while hunting chukars, which will be covered in another chapter.

## 20 | Wilson Snipe

In the early Twenties Orval Overall, the old Chicago Cubs' pitcher and a member of the Twenty-Eight Gun Club, invited me to shoot ducks on their grounds near Allensworth, Tulare County. It was a fine club and I, of course, was happy to go. The club grounds were all of Section 28, and consisted of an even 640 acres. The well was on the southeast corner with a reservoir. It was an artesian well. The water ran continuously, a fairly good stream. In fact, it kept the grounds wet and partly flooded between the well and the first pond, some one-third mile west of the clubhouse, as well as all other shooting ponds on the Club.

The ponds were built shallow to attract pintail or sprig ducks, and it certainly worked on those grounds. The blinds were situated so that shooting at one location seldom interfered with the shooting at any other blind. In those days the limit of ducks was 25 and it was no trouble to bag your limit. Your only problem was to give them the proper lead. That morning the sprig were coming in by the hundreds; one bunch after another. While other ducks were in the air, we ignored them and took the sprig.

This type of duck ordinarily worked later in the morning, so I waited them out, and it was nearly 10:30 before I picked up my limit of 25, mostly cocks, and headed for the clubhouse. Now 25 pintails weigh some 60 pounds. So after getting them on my shoulder, I took the direct route, which was through the wet marsh, and it was tough going, but I noticed something. The

## Wilson Snipe

Wilson snipe were in that marsh also, and by the hundreds. My spirits were high, and the load was not nearly so heavy. I reached my destination really rested up and found two boxes of number nine shot in a 20 gauge load and I was fixed. I waited until the other shooters were in and told them of my plans. No one was interested in shooting Wilson snipe and I could not figure the reason, because it is a fine target and a very palatable bird for the table.

The birds usually flush close to the shooter, but at times they seem very wild and flush farther away. This day they were on their good behavior and were flushing close. I had a field day. They take off with a "tweet-tweet" and zigzag and are not an easy target. Take the right zig or the left zag or you will not have many for dinner.

I will tell you of another trick I have learned. If you stand still and wait a few moments, many times they will return to the same spot from which they flushed, and they are a much easier target. It did not take long for me to fill my limit of 25 birds, and I do not think I was over a quarter of a mile from the clubhouse. When I returned I tried to be a gentleman and offered to share my luck with Overall and other members of the club. Of course, they were gentlemen enough to refuse, especially under the circumstances. It was a day I will long remember. A limit of 25 sprig and a limit of Wilson snipe, and all before noon.

Years later, Dick Chatten and I were hunting quail on the ranch of Harry Spaulding, an old high school schoolmate. We had finished bagging our limit of 15 quail in his vineyard and were returning to the ranch house. I noticed the "tweet-tweet" of the Wilson snipe and birds flying over his 40 acres of permanent pasture.

It had been raining for several days and the birds had come in from the north. Chatten had shot a few at the Widgeon Club, west of Delano, California, but without too much success, mainly because they had little marshland, such as the Twenty-Eight Gun Club, where I had shot them previously, had. We decided to try our luck and waded without rubber boots in the slush, muck and water for an additional two hours and were compensated with a limit of 15 each of those wonderful targets and fine table birds. If you are out after pheasants or quail and following a rain, do not overlook a permanent pasture. The snipe may be there, and they are worth your effort for sport or table. It is a fine bird.

## 21 | Upland Plover

Another game bird is the upland plover, similar in some respects, but very different in habitat to the Wilson snipe. The upland plover reminds me of the Kildeer, sometimes known as the Kildee, very familiar to most people residing in this area. This bird is migrant and in the fall and winter lands in the arid area, such as the Lost Hills in Kern County and the West Side of Fresno and Kings Counties.

About 1920 J. Newt Young, former supervisor of Tulare County and an ardent hunter, a fine upland game shot and an expert fly fisherman, and I decided to try a quail shoot in the Bitterwater Canyon area in San Luis Obispo County. We knew that Orval Overall, the old Chicago Cubs pitcher, and his associates were boring for oil in the Lost Hills area. Since Orval was a shooting partner of each of us, we decided to go by and see how they were getting along. We happened to land in camp just about dinner time, and because of their hospitality we were asked to stay for dinner.

It was a long way to a restaurant, so we decided to accept their invitation without much persuasion. After dinner they suggested that we stay overnight with them inasmuch as they needed two more to have a poker game. We again could find no reason to refuse. We did not get much sleep, but took about $160 from them just to pay expenses. Newt was a pretty good poker player, and I had beginner's luck.

After breakfast the next morning, Al Askin, who was helping on the lease, offered to drive us over to Bitterwater and share our quail shoot. We started west over the plains when, much to our surprise, we noticed that the area was alive with high-flying upland game birds which Young identified as upland plover. They were in the area by the thousands, and everywhere. We were not sure that the season was open, but there were so many that we decided to get a few.

In those days we had running boards on each side of the automobile. Evidently Askin had some experience hunting upland plover because he said, "Get on the running board, I'll do the driving." He would drive "hell bent for election" into a bunch of birds, then put on the brakes. We would jump off and wait, when after a short interval, here they would come, and it was fast and furious and interesting shooting.

About an hour later, I was out with my dog retrieving plover, when I noticed Young and Askin run for the car, jump in and head toward Bakersfield, leaving me with all the plover -- Young's, Askin's and my own -- in my shooting coat; because I had my dog making the retrieve, and they knew the stranger in the on-coming automobile was the game warden. They did not know that the season was open or what the limit was, and I had all the birds!

The stranger drove up and wanted to know the road to McKittrick. What a relief to me and my dog Sport. I think every good dog my father or I ever owned was named Sport. We passed the time of day, and the stranger wished me well and headed in the direction I had advised. After he drove away, my two shooting partners returned with a sheepish smile and gave me the horse laugh. After a good cussing by myself, we divided the birds and headed for Bitterwater. We arrived about 11:30, loaded our guns, cast off the dog and within 10 minutes we were in the birds. They were everywhere; in the low sagebrush and greasewood, literally by the hundreds. The limit at that time was 25 per day, and after the first few shots, the birds went to cover, so we had one point after another, each shooter,

## Upland Plover

shooting side by side, Newt with a 20 gauge gun and Al Askin with a 12 gauge and I with a 20 gauge Parker. We had no trouble filling our limits within a couple of hours.

It was just one point after another. A single and then a double, each shooter taking his turn, regardless of what it was.

We had not thought of being hungry, but were back at the car just before two o'clock for lunch; each with his limit of 25 quail. We did what was necessary and headed for the Lost Hills for another session of the guessing game. Well, it developed so after dinner we were at it again, but Young and Buckman did not do quite as well.

We returned to Visalia with limits of quail and upland plover. Joe Barboni, manager of what is now Security Pacific National Bank, and George C. Cobb, the dealer for the Dodge automobile and an ardent duck hunter, were in the same room at the Visalia Hospital. We knew they would enjoy some plover, which incidentally is one of the finest table birds. Mrs. Buckman did her usual job, and we delivered a dinner that evening fit for kings. Neither knew what he was eating, but they did know it was tops.

## 22 | Sandhill Cranes

My earliest recollection of game in Central California was when I was only a youngster. Mother would put my brother and me to bed and we would lie and listen to the wild-sounding, trumpet-like calls of the sandhill cranes and the honking of the geese coming down from the north to spend the winter in Central California and again in the spring going north for their nesting season. While there are some two dozen species of cranes in the world, there are only two which occur in California -- the sandhill and a little brown crane. Each of these cranes are grey with red caps and are cousins of the extremely rare white whooping crane found in the United States only along the west side of the Mississippi River valley.

There was an open season on the crane during my younger days, but market hunting nearly doomed the cranes to extinction. But now, under complete protection with a closed season, about 15,000 of these stately birds annually winter in California, arriving in Northern California as early as September.

From 3,000 to 6,000 converge and remain in the delta of the Sacramento and San Joaquin Rivers. Other smaller flocks of a few hundred each are found in Colusa County to as far south as the Carriso Planes west of Bakersfield.

About 3,500 of the total number are the greater sandhills, but since the sandhill and the little brown have almost identical plumage, from the sequence of moults to adult plumage, they

# Sandhill Cranes

are difficult to distinguish. The sandhill is taller, however -- nearly five feet in height.

With the above information before us, imagine the proportion of this bird that kept my brother and me awake so many nights in my childhood. They were in this valley by the thousands and thousands. I recall discussing the sandhill with an old market hunter, who told me of shooting them by the dozens and shipping them to the market in San Francisco at a very nominal figure.

The cranes are dry-land feeders. They nest on the ground and prefer treeless marshes in which to nest and large, unfenced grasslands and prairies where they could graze for food in the security of distance. They are extremely wary, so caution must be used when approaching them, for at any time a sharp-eyed sentinel may voice an alarm and the great birds will leap into the air and be gone. The cranes stay at the winter ground until February. Then, overpowered by the urge to go to the breeding grounds, they take to the skies. Some flocks will spiral up and up until almost out of sight, with only the lingering sound of that strange call to proclaim their departure.

There is some nesting in Northeastern California, but most of them go further north. Studies made at the Malheur Refuge in Oregon show that the area used by each pair averages about six acres and is defended by each pair. The nests are constructed by both male and female, and some nests are large enough to support the crane if waters rise and cause it to float.

Egg laying commences in mid-April. There are two, and occasionally three, large, pale olive-colored eggs, marked by spots of buffy brown. The eggs are laid several days apart and both parents help to incubate the eggs. The first egg is hatched a day or so before the second, and they leave the nest as soon as the second chick is dry.

The parents keep the young 15 to 50 feet apart for weeks so the older chick cannot assault the smaller bird. The young stay with the parents and are fed by regurgitation for several months. They do not fly until they are nearly as large as the adult birds, but they walk long distances and run and hide to escape their enemies.

At the Malheur Refuge there is considerable nest destruction by ravens, raccoons, skunks and coyotes, but as long as we retain some place for these birds to winter, strange sounds and curious antics of cranes should continue to herald the changing of the seasons.

My next brush with the sandhill crane was in Regina, Saskatchewan, when we were obtaining our hunting license for our trip to that area in 1946. As the game officer handed us our licenses, he looked us straight in the eye and said, "I want to admonish you not to shoot our wild turkeys." I looked him straight in the eye and said, "That is something I believe you do not have here," and he laughed and said, "No, but we do have the sandhill cranes, and are trying to protect them." They were safe as far as our party was concerned. We shook hands and departed for Moosejaw.

After all these years, the sandhill has made a comeback, until now there is an open season in New Mexico, according to *Scoreboard West*. Opening day for the lesser sandhill crane is an exciting affair at Roswell, New Mexico. In fact, Roswell is known as the New Mexico crane-hunting capitol. Thousands of cranes winter and rest at the nearby Bitter Lake National Refuge. They have almost a 90-day season, a limit of three and six in possession.

# 23 | Rambling Memories

Short sketches of some shoots and other conditions may give you an idea of the game situation 75 years ago and later.

I will never forget a shoot on doves on the Chowchilla River north of Fresno, some 60 years ago. Automobiles were just coming into use for transportation. I had access to one so accepted an invitation to partake in a shoot east of where the town of Chowchilla now stands. The whole country at that time was farmed to grain, wheat mostly, but some barley. The water level was only six or seven feet from the surface, and there was one water hole on the Chowchilla River for some miles.

We reached the water hole about 3:30 in the afternoon and the doves had started to water, but my host advised me to wait until we were well settled because we were in for a sight and could get all the birds we wanted to get in a very few minutes. He knew the superintendent of the old people's home in Fresno and had promised to furnish the home with a dove feed, and I had been invited to assist in furnishing the doves.

We watched them come in until about 4:30, when our nervous systems could not take it much longer. They were there, not by the hundreds, but by the thousands. We put our double-barrels together and took our stands, my host above the water hole and I just below. The birds fell in the sand on the bottom of the creek and were easily visible so we did not pick up until we thought we had enough to give the home a good feed.

The shooting was so fast and the evening so warm it was necessary to cool the barrels off by placing them under the water. This worked very well but it was necessary to be sure that we had the surplus water out of the tubes before we again started to shoot. It was fast and furious, and it seemed that I could not miss. Of course, this was not true. I wish I had counted my shells so that I could have known my average, which was pretty good at that. We picked up and filled a flour sack with doves for their feed, and were they glad to get them!

During the early Twenties we made several hunting trips to what is known as the "Pocket" near O'Neils Station in Madera County. A very fine Mexican family by the name of Topping lived in the area and he, too, was a quail hunter, and a good one. We made arrangements with them to take care of us for two or three days of quail shoots. We would hunt all day after a late breakfast and come in to an early Spanish feed prepared by Mrs. Topping. It was great, and her Spanish dinners were tops. The "Pocket" area was about the best quail country I can remember. The quail were everywhere, out of one covey into another all day long. There was a weed we called wild broomcorn that grew quite plentifully in the area. It was some 18 inches high and quite thick, perfect cover for quail and dog work.

I well remember one shoot when our "better halves" went with us, and we were about two miles from the house when the heavens opened up suddenly and we were soaked. After that, the wives stayed home and played bridge.

The limit was 25, which we had no trouble getting but could give away to Mr. Topping's neighbors without breaking the game laws.

Just to prove that the game supply is not depleted and that there are a few places where an ample supply still exists, a few years ago we were going to Malheur County, Oregon to hunt pheasant and Hungarian partridges when a friend of mine learned of our trip and the owner of the Alvord Ranch on the

# Rambling Memories

east side of the Steens Mountains in Harney County invited us to shoot a day or two on his beautiful cattle ranch.

It was "too good to be true." In one day, we had limits of quail, Hungarian partridges, pheasants and Mallard ducks. It was fabulous. We hunted quail and pheasant together and at the same time. We went up into the low sloping hills of the Steens Mountains for the partridges when we noticed the ducks coming in to feed on the flats below us. We went down and found a 10-acre field of barley that had not been harvested, where we stood in the sunflowers and shot Mallard ducks. There were so many that we only shot the drakes. We left the game for the mess house of the Alvord Ranch, thanked the representative of our host and left for Ontario, the county seat of Malheur County, where we were to hunt pheasants and Hungarian partridges.

A few years later Forrest Kerr and I were invited by Lyle Hagler to again hunt in Harney County, Oregon on Wild Horse Creek, near Andrews. To reach there, go to Winnemucca, Nevada then north to Denio, Fields and Andrews. We met our host there and headed west to the Harry Blair Ranch, which was a sportsman's paradise. When we drove up to the ranch house the pheasants were thick in the front yard, eating apples. We rested the balance of the first day but the next day obtained limits of quail and pheasants in less than two hours. The next day we drove south to Fields, where there was a road west into the Steens Mountains which we took, and shot limits of chukars in less than two hours. The birds had really taken hold and were there by the hundreds. It was there that we found out that birds fly downhill; they will not fly uphill. We put hunters in the canyon below and drove the jeep into the covey and flushed them. The men in the canyon received some good shooting. We saw many small flocks of sage hens, but they were out of season at this time of the year.

Many deer hunters go into that area for deer. The Steens Mountains are famous for the deer hunter. In fact, I killed my only buck while hunting quail on Wild Horse Creek with a 20 gauge Parker and 1⅛ ounce of shot. The buck came right at me, down the creek. He evidently did not see me. I stood still until it was very near me. I shot it between the eyes at a distance of less than five feet, and there was my first and only forked horn.

May I suggest that if you go to this country you either go in a camper or arrange for hunting privileges and accommodations before reaching the area. There are some fine people there. Pay them well, and you will more than get your money's worth.

I will never forget a quail shoot in the Early Twenties. I was returning from Tulare when, as I was passing Mooney Grove, a covey of quail of some 300 birds flew out of the grove in front of the car and settled in a vineyard on the west side of the road. I knew the owner of the land so stopped and obtained permission, then hurried home to get my gun, dog and a shooter to accompany me. I will not disclose his name because of what happened. I had hunted with him on other occasions and he had always controlled his temper and had been a gentleman.

We flushed the birds soon after entering the vineyard, and they went to cover on the west end. We were having a field day when we got separated and I heard a great deal of swearing, saw my partner jumping up and down with the words "I'll sell this dog for $15." This after he had told me he had been offered $250 for the "Lady that is known as Lou."

I walked over. He was jumping on Lou, who had had a bad day and had broken two or three points. I said, "Did I hear you correctly?" He answered, "You sure did." I could not stand the cruelty so reached into my hip pocket, pulled out my wallet and handed him the $15 with, "Now don't touch that dog, I own her." I pulled out a leash, took my new dog and put her in the car! Not another word was said. I did not think he would go through with his threat but he did, so we finished our shoot with 25 birds each, the limit in those days, and went home. He thanked me for the shoot and went into his house. I went to mine with my Peggy, who had a wonderful afternoon, with point after point, and my new acquisition, still chuckling. As I went into the house and met Mrs. Buckman I burst out laughing and she said, "Have you been drinking?" I answered in the negative and told her the story, which she does not believe to this day.

There I was with two dogs, one of which I had no use for. My Peggy did all that any good setter could be expected to do. So the next morning I met Jim Fluty on the street. Jim was our chief of police, and we had hunted together on many occasions. He wanted a good dog, a real bird dog, so he took over my $15 investment. Everybody was happy, including the original owner, who never peeped as long as he lived. Fluty shot over Lou for some years and finally gave the dog to Frank Blessing, who hunted over the "Lady known as Lou" until she reached the age of 12 and passed away.

In those days there were enough birds and the season was long enough to be able to train, or have trained, a good bird dog. There is simply no excuse, except pure laziness or no cooperation at home, which of course made it hard for peace and comfort. I was never troubled with that problem as Mrs. Buckman was always very considerate of my wishes in this respect. We could have shot over our limits that afternoon without Peggy or Lou, but it would not have been near the sport. It would, however, have been more pleasant had my shooting partner not lost his temper.

About the year 1919 Arthur Crites, the banker and super sportsman of Bakersfield, invited Newt Young, the famous Upland gunshot and supervisor of this county at the time, and me to be his guests over the weekend at his duck club on Goose Lake in Kern County. It was near the end of the quail season, so Newt and yours truly decided to accept the invitation and wind up the quail season in Bitterwater Canyon on the Coast Range.

I well remember that breakfast at his club and the tramp to our blinds with our host as guide, and it was well that we had a guide. The ice in the ponds was about ½ inch. It was under 20 degrees, and there we were without our red flannels. We were directed to our blinds into which we climbed in the cold because no one had told us to take a can or two of canned heat, the trade name of which is Sterno. It is a great product. They tell me some hobos strain it through a cloth and drink the alcohol. I cannot vouch for the veracity of this report because I would much rather use it to keep warm in a duck blind.

It was a great shoot, limiting on sprig and Mallards, but we had to break the ice to pick up the birds. It was a sight to see an old Mallard sit down and skid for some yards and then stand up, shake his head and tail and wonder just what had happened.

Some years of my younger life were spent on the Buckman homestead of my grandfather located on Outside Creek west and north of Exeter. It was a sportsman's paradise -- quail, duck, doves and cottontail rabbits everywhere. I was about 12 years old but really loved a shotgun. My father taught me to be careful so would permit me to go hunting by myself. I did not have to go far. If I wanted to shoot some ducks I would go down to Outside Creek in the evening. The woodducks would be flying up and down the creek. I could always bring back a dinner for the family, or I could stalk the Blain ditch which went through the Blain field northeast from our house. It seemed that I could always find a couple of Mallard loafing on the ditch. I would crawl on my stomach a long way to get a shot.

The quail were everywhere. They would flush into and along a fence line where it was just a question of how many I wanted

# Rambling Memories

for dinner. There was an 80-acre field east in front of the house with valley oaks over most of the area, some of which had been cut and corded for firewood. This was an ideal place for quail to hide and was also a wonderful place to work my father's dog Sport.

I will never forget a winter when heavy rains flooded the creek and drove the cottontail rabbit out into the carefully corded firewood. They were there by the hundreds so my brother Ray and I thought of the bright idea of killing and dressing them, for which we received a few cents a dozen from the neighbors. It worked fine until the owner of the land and wood, my uncle A. J. Buckman, came over and took my father and showed him where we had knocked over perhaps a hundred tiers of his wood while catching the rabbits. We did not hunt or play until the wood was re-corded, which took all the after-school playtime and Saturdays for the balance of the winter. It was a good lesson but a dear one for us. The next year we spent trapping raccoons. We had the side of the barn plastered with skins drying, for which we received the big sum of 30 cents each.

One day while mother and sister were in Visalia, we returned from school and found father alone. Our home had burned to the ground and he was sitting in a rocking chair with my gun across his lap and a sewing machine beside him, all he had been able to save with but one arm to work with. The next day we built a platform and put up a tent when it started to rain. It rained steadily for about two weeks. The tent leaked, so we had stew instead of fried meat.

Soon afterwards we moved to Exeter, which was not clear out of the game area. Dad had saved my Parker shotgun, so on Saturday I hunted the Outside Ditch for ducks and the hog-wallow plains where we could crawl on our stomachs to get a shot at a few ducks. This reminds me of a story which I once heard of a letter received by Mr. Olen of the Winchester Arms

Company. "If you had crawled on your stomach for half a mile to get a shot and had your shell be a dud, you would make better ammunition." And they did just that!

Tulare Lake in 1907 was a wild fowl paradise. Frank Carl and I drove two miles west of Corcoran in Kings County, swam a 20-foot drainage ditch, walked two miles into the lake without getting wet over our knees, broke down some tules to sit on and put out a few decoys. They came by the hundreds, Mallards, Sprig (they are also called pintail), Spoolbill, Widgeon and Teal. It did not take long to kill 50 birds apiece, and we took only Mallards and Sprig.

Can you imagine -- we could not carry them! Carl was frail and I was a junior in high school. We had a council of war, took off our shirts, tore them into strips, tied the ducks together and floated them to shore.

We threw them across the drainage ditch, loaded up and returned to Visalia with 100 big, beautiful ducks. But when we tried to give some away they wanted us to pick them.

# 24 | Clubs and Shooting Preserves

Over the past 75 years I have watched the steady decline of our game resources and the steady closing of property to the sportsmen with signs of "No Hunting" and "No Trespassing" until the individual who is now in the area and does not know the landowner just has no place to hunt.

The closing of property to hunters has been brought about to a great extent by the sportsmen themselves. They have torn down fences, left gates open, left beer cans and lunch papers on the premises until the landowner has almost been forced to close his property to protect himself. Not all of the sportsmen are guilty of the above, but a few have made it tough for the individual who does try to be a gentleman.

The time is about here when it will be impossible to go bird shooting unless you are a member of a private shooting club or go to a commercial shooting preserve.

Private leasing of shooting areas is against the principle of many hunters, who are of the opinion that game is owned by the public, not the owner of the land, but remember, it is the owner who has to repair his fence and pick up the beer cans. It has been my privilege to have been a member of a private shooting club for many years, and it has worked out to a distinct advantage for all concerned. We have a place where we can go and hunt without obligation to anyone for permission. We post the property and take care of it as though it were our own.

This shows what can be accomplished on a private club with a triplex (quail brush) for feed and cover.

## Clubs and Shooting Preserves

It happens to be an area where my father hunted with his shooting partners over 100 years ago. The owner is relieved of the constant requests for permission to hunt the property. They tell me that they really like the arrangement.

There are a few problems that must be observed with a private quail club. Membership should be kept to a low level. Guests should not be permitted even though you would give a great deal to be able to take a friend on a good quail shoot. In addition, the property should not be overshot. It is so easy to spook the California quail and have them leave their habitat.

I am convinced that good hunting, with guaranteed game, will replace our dwindling natural hunting with commercial shooting preserves. It is so much easier and less time-consuming to get to a good preserve than it is to go to Idaho or South Dakota. I have done both and believe the preserves to be the answer from any standpoint -- birds, time, ultimate cost and comfort. Don't sell the ringneck short. It is wild when released and gives you a good shot when flushed.

A good, well-operated preserve with the proper cover and steady dogs will give you the shooting and the day of sport you are looking for. You can usually find a good dog on a shooting preserve, so it is not absolutely necessary to own your own. This is another advantage of shooting on the so-called synthetic hunting ground. Another advantage is synthetic reserve hunters may ride or walk as they choose. This permits elderly persons or even those handicapped to enjoy a day in the field.

One of the big advantages of preserve hunting is the fact that you can pursue so many varieties of game. Besides the pheasant I have hunted the California quail, the Bobwhite, the chukar, the guinea hen and the wild turkey, all of which give you good dog work while hunting them.

Remember, too, the usual season for hunting on a commercial shooting preserve is six months, consisting of October, November, December, January, February and March of each

*A point! Chuckar hunting on the Kern-Delta Shooting Preserve, Bakersfield, California.*

year. This is long enough to train a dog or for the sportsman to follow his hobby. I also must mention the fact that most well organized preserves have facilities for cleaning your game after it has been bagged. This, to me, is a big help after hunting in the field for a few hours. A small fee is charged but it is well worth the fee, and the game can go home ready for the freezer or stove.

From the information given, there are plenty of reasons why the preserve should be successful, and with proper attention I am firmly convinced that the day will come when a great percentage of our hunting will be done by this method.

# Appendix | A Few Recipes

To assist you when one of your sportsman friends favors you with a mess of game, I give you the following:

## STEAMED DOVES

In a dutch oven or heavy aluminum kettle with a tight lid, melt half a cube of butter and add one bell pepper, chopped, 3 medium onions, sliced, and 1 large clove of garlic, chopped fine. Let cook gently a few minutes. Then put in 10 or 12 doves which have been cleaned thoroughly, arranging so they are not more than two deep in the kettle. Add 2 cupfuls boiling water and 2 slices of bacon which have been cut into small bits and fried light brown. Cover and cook slowly for an hour. Then add Worcestershire sauce and continue cooking, adding water as it cooks away. When doves are tender, make a thickened gravy by browning 3 tablespoons of flour and adding 1 cup milk. When smooth, pour into kettle with doves. Just before taking up, add 1 tablespoon catsup and sherry wine to suit taste. Chicken may also be cooked this way.

## DOVES

When the day comes and you have had a poor shoot or when your sportsman friend has given you only a few doves, here is a recipe that is a favorite of Mrs. Buckman:

Pinch of thyme and rosemary
Parsley -- 1 teaspoon chopped
1 can mushrooms (4 oz.)

1 cup white wine
1 teaspoon salt

Cut doves along back and butterfly. Roll in flour and brown in butter. Add thyme, rosemary and chopped parsley. Cover and cook slowly for 15 minutes. Add chopped onion, mushrooms with the liquid and wine.

Cover and simmer for one hour or longer. Add salt about 5 minutes before removing from heat. Add more wine if you would like more gravy. Add during the cooking period.

## DOVES WITH GREEN PEAS

Clean the birds, raise the skin over the breasts and insert as much dressing, seasoned to taste, as possible. Tie bacon over the breasts and dredge lightly with seasoned flour. Arrange in a buttered baking dish; add diluted consomme to cover the bottom about one-half inch. Cover and place in a 325-degree oven. When the birds are almost tender, remove cover and permit them to brown. Remove bacon strip at the same time. Place birds on a warm platter, add a little heavy cream and dry white wine to the pan juice, bring to a boil, correct seasoning, pour over the birds. Serve with green peas.

## BAKED QUAIL

Plan on one quail per person, but have seconds available.

Clean birds, wipe inside and out with a damp cloth. Stuff with a dressing of chopped mushrooms, bread crumbs, butter, cream, seasoned to taste; truss, rub the exterior with salt and butter, place on a bed of bacon slices, add just a little water to the baking pan, roast for 30 minutes in a 325-degree oven or until the birds are brown. Fifteen minutes before the birds are done, add one-half cup heavy cream to each bird in the roasting pan.

## A Few Recipes

### QUAIL SUPREME

Dress quail as you would chicken, leaving birds whole. Rub inside with fine salad oil, sprinkle with salt and pepper, then stuff with chopped celery, bell pepper, onion and carrot, with tiny bit of minced garlic.

Make French dressing of 1 tablespoon vinegar to 5 tablespoons salad oil, ¼ teaspoon A-1 or Worcestershire sauce and 2 tablespoons catsup; salt and pepper to taste. Put a teaspoon of this dressing in each bird and place birds in an open roasting pan.

Heat oven for 10 minutes, having control at 550 degrees (extremely hot, if no oven control). When very hot, put birds in and let cook for five minutes. Pour some French dressing over breast of each bird and cook for 10 minutes. Baste again with French dressing, place short strip bacon on breast of each bird, cook five minutes longer. Oven should be kept at 550 degrees at all times. Remove dressing and serve quail on thin rounds of toast, pouring a bit of hot French dressing over each.

### ROAST PHEASANT

Clean and dress three well-hung pheasants. Rub with sweet butter on the exterior, rinse out the cavities with 2 tablespoons of brandy each, season with salt, pepper, a little crumbled tarragon, place on a rack in an uncovered roasting pan. Roast for 15 minutes in a 325-degree oven. Add 6 tablespoons of Madeira to the juices in the pan; roast for 30 minutes, basting every 10 minutes. Fifteen minutes before serving, place 6 rounds of rye bread in the pan to brown in the juices. Place pheasants on a bed of watercress, surround with bread slices and garnish with lemon slices.

### PHEASANT FRICASSEE

The next time you get a pheasant -- either hunting or as a gift from a sportsman friend --

Clean and dress, cut it up and cook it like chicken fricassee with dumplings!

## ROAST WILD TURKEY

Now that we have an open season in California on the wild turkey, you may need a recipe. Here it is!

The wild turkey, a lean and muscular bird, requires heat, larding and frequent basting. Stuff with highly spiced fat sausage, chopped onion, a pinch of sage, chopped mushrooms, bread crumbs, one chopped hard apple. Truss.

Rub exterior with salt and butter. Drape fat pork or bacon strips on the breast. Wrap thin strips around the legs and cover the wings with them also. Place the prepared turkey in a 325-degree oven, breast up. There's only one rule: Roast until tender. Baste frequently with a mixture of lemon juice and melted butter, and with dry sherry in the final half-hour of cooking. The bird is tender when the leg joint will bend easily on moving it up and down. Remove from the oven and cut off the trussing strings. Discard the larding. Let stand for five or 10 minutes before serving.

## WINE GOOSE (WILD)

Cut wild goose into pieces for stewing and put pieces into an enamelware pan or a crock or glass bowl. Add one large onion, sliced, 5 cloves of garlic, 1 red dry pepper, 4 bay leaves, 5 whole cloves and a generous amount of salt and black pepper. Pour over all sufficient claret or sauterne to cover. Cover with plate and weight down to keep the meat submerged in liquid. Let stand 24 to 72 hours. Turn whole mixture into kettle with tight-fitting lid and add 2 tablespoons dry mushrooms which have been washed thoroughly. Let simmer slowly for 1½ hours. Then cook briskly until meat is tender, adding no water unless necessary.

# A Few Recipes

## WILD DUCK AND VENISON
Cook as with Wine Goose (Wild).

## WILD DUCK (RARE)
Do not cook for at least a day after killing, or it will be tough.

Clean and dress as usual, being sure to cut out oil sacs above tail.

Into each large duck put 2 kernels of garlic, slashed. Then fill cavity tightly with celery leaves and onions. Heat oven as hot as possible (set control at 600 degrees). Then put in ducks in dry open roasting pan. Let roast for five minutes. Then baste with French dressing, place strip of bacon on each breast and put back in oven for five minutes. Keep oven heat very high throughout entire cooking, which is 15 minutes for teal and 20 for sprig. Remove stuffing before serving. Garnish with slices or eighths of lemon dipped in paprika. -- From *Ducks Unlimited* Magazine.

## ROAST DUCK
Stuffing: Combine 1 cup chopped celery, 1 cup chopped onion, 2 cups water. Set aside for 15 to 20 minutes. Combine 4 cups cubed dry bread, ¼ teaspoon pepper, 1 teaspoon salt, 1 teaspoon poultry seasoning, ½ teaspoon sage.

Combine with celery, onion and water mixture, adding enough water until dressing is barely moist.

Rub the ducks lightly with salt and pepper. Stuff with moist dressing. Put ducks in a roasting pan no larger than two ducks. Add one cup of water and cover. Roast at 325 degrees for two hours. Remove from oven; fasten one slice of onion on each duck breast with a toothpick. Roast two hours longer until duck is tender. -- Mrs. Henry Dilly, Hastings, Nebraska.

## SKILLET COOT
Peel skin back and remove the breast meat and legs within a few hours after the coots are shot. This gives four pieces from

each bird, two drumsticks and the breast halves. Wash thoroughly and remove most of the fat. Roll pieces in seasoned flour (pepper and onion salt seasoning). Cook for about an hour at low temperature (just about simmer), in electric skillet with a generous amount of vegetable oil. -- C. Holden Brink, Norris, Tennessee.

### OLD DUCK HUNTER'S ROAST DUCK

Take two or more ducks of any kind. Season lightly inside and out with salt and pepper. Stuff each duck with sauerkraut. Pour one big glass of sherry wine over ducks. Cook in a bag at 400 degrees for one hour. Be sure to punch 5 to 6 holes in the top of the bag. Serve with lemon and cayenne red pepper to taste. -- Arch Medlin, Visalia, California.

### A DUCK HUNTER'S ROAST DUCK IN A HURRY

Take 2 sprig or 2 mallard ducks. Lightly add salt, pepper and seasoning inside and outside. Stuff with pieces of apple, carrots and onions. Slice breast of birds and put in mustard and cayenne pepper. Pour one glass of sherry wine over ducks and in roasting pan. Bake 1 hour in 400-degree oven. Best you have ever eaten and wild, too, in taste. -- Arch Medlin, Visalia, California.

The wild flavor some ducks have goes down the drain -- not to the table -- if you fix them this way:

The time-honored method of preparing wild ducks for the table is to pluck, wax, roast and serve them under dim candlelight so the pinfeathers will not show. Concealed also under the dim lights are the feathers which each shot carries into the meat. True, ducks prepared by this method with their brown, crispy skin taste fine to the tired and ravenously hungry hunter, but if you asked the patient housewife, who spent nearly the whole day trying to make them presentable for the table, the

## A Few Recipes

story might be different. Often, she would gladly settle for hamburger.

Actually, late-season ducks, which are completely out of the pinfeather stage, look beautiful and are excellent when prepared with the skins intact. This is often true, but it is not always the case, for there are times when the appearance and flavor of wild ducks are definitely enhanced by the removal of the skins. These times are five in number and are as follows:

First, early-season ducks should be skinned because they invariably are in the pinfeather stage, with many feathers under the skin that are absolutely impossible to remove by any plucking and waxing method yet devised.

Second, ducks badly shot up should be skinned, because each shot carries feathers into the meat which cannot be seen and removed unless the ducks are skinned.

Third, if ducks are to be frozen for a long period of time, the layer of fat directly underneath the skin turns rancid and imparts a strong, "wild" flavor to the entire duck. This layer always adheres to the skin and when the skin is removed, so is the fat. This point does not apply to ducks to be frozen for only a few weeks before cooking, but it definitely is true of ducks which are to be kept in a freezer for months.

The fourth reason for skinning ducks is to remove the fishy or strong taste of certain species. Even the best ducks in certain localities will have a strong flavor sometimes. Most of this strong taste is found in the fatty tissue directly under the skin, and when the skin is removed so also the tissue and objectionable taste. For example, even merganzers become quite edible if skinned and prepared by the prescribed methods.

The fifth and last reason given for skinning ducks is because it is much faster, easier, and cleaner than plucking them. Anyone who has tried to pluck a duck in an apartment knows exactly the significance of this point. One is reminded of it by floating feathers from one duck season to the next. True, there will be some loose feathers and down when skinning ducks, but they by no means present the problem encountered if the plucking method is used. Here is the way we do it.

The first step is the actual skinning. After you've severed the wings and legs at the joints, insert a knife under the skin of the breast and cut down the center. Peel the skin away, helping it separate from the flesh with a razor. As you progress, it becomes easier. When the skin is off, remove the entrails and wash inside and out well. Clean out each shot hole individually.

After the ducks are skinned and washed comes the important soaking. Place a pan of water with about two tablespoons of salt and one of soda for each gallon of water and let the ducks soak for at least 10 hours. This will draw out the gamy taste. You can be generous with the ingredients since washing in cold water will remove any salt or soda taste. Now the ducks are ready to be cooked or frozen.

Next comes the stuffing. Slice apples, onions, celery and carrots four ways and fill each body cavity. You don't have to close the opening, as the stuffing will be discarded. Its purpose is to absorb strong flavor and add its own flavors to the meat. Bacon strips over the breasts prevent drying out while you bake uncovered for one hour at 325 degrees; two hours at 300 degrees. Serve with wild rice, salad and red wine.

## "Green Lodge" Recipe for
## MUD HEN STEW a la "HUNTER"

Skin the birds (not pick them) and soak a few hours (or all night) in water to which has been added a little salt.

Then take the birds out of this salt water and put in the kettle with enough cold water inside to cover them.

When this water comes to a boil, take the birds out and throw away the water.

Put the birds in the pot, add one half a pound salt pork, cut in dice, cover with hot water, and let boil about one hour.

# A Few Recipes

Then add:
- Half a dozen whole cloves
- One medium sized onion cut up fine
- Half a bay leaf
- Salt and pepper to taste
- Peeled potatoes as desired

Put one teaspoon full of curry powder and two tablespoons of white flour in a cup and mix with water.

Add these to stew about one half hour before taking up stew. Serve with boiled rice as side dish.

And then put it where it will do the most good.

-- W. W. Richards

# NOTIS!

trespassers will B persecuted to the full extent of 2 mungrel dogs which never was over sochible to strangers & 1 dubble bril shot gun which aint loded with sofa pillors. Dam if I aint gitten tired of this hell raisin on my place.

— B. Griscom